Changed By Beholding HIM

Changed By Beholding HIM

"Leaving us an example, that ye should follow his steps."
I Peter 2:21

Newton C. Conant

A BARBOUR BOOK

Quotations from:

The King James Version of the Bible. Minor changes have occasionally been made in the text in keeping with modern usage.

The New Scofield Reference Bible. Copyright © 1967 by Oxford University Press, Inc. Reprinted by permission.

Power Through Prayer by E. M. Bounds. Zondervan Publishing House. Reprinted by permission.

Christianity Today editorial "Demonism on the March," February 17, 1967. Copyright © 1967 by *Christianity Today*; reprinted by permission.

Love Not the World by Watchman Nee. Britain, Victory Press; USA., Christian Literature Crusade. Used by permission.

ISBN 1-55748-461-9

Copyright © 1972 Christian Literature Crusade

Published by Barbour and Company, Inc., P.O. Box 719, 1810 Barbour Drive, Uhrichsville, OH 44683

Printed in the U.S.A.

Foreword

It is rare that words written in our generation speak to the Christian's heart with such a quiet yet compelling urgency. The warm, inviting ring of truth is on every page, and surely the reader will not escape the quickening of the heart's hunger for God.

The realities of this book were learned and lived by a quiet, self-effacing servant of Christ in a pastorate of nearly thirty-nine years in a difficult, deteriorating section of Camden, New Jersey.

These realities took flesh in a congregation of men and women that grew from a handful of five to a thrilling company of redeemed souls who love the Lord Jesus Christ. These certainties moved many young men and women out into lives of effective Christian service, and released hundreds of God's servants from frustration, despair, fruitlessness, and defeat. The realities which this book presents so warmly and winsomely, and yet so urgently, are at the heart core of the most desperate need of the church today.

We counted it a privilege to have heard these messages first preached at Harvey Cedars Bible Conference. Great blessing accompanied their presentation. Now we enthusiastically commend them to a wider audience through this book.

Albert W. Oldham, Director
Harvey Cedars Bible Conference
Harvey Cedars, New Jersey

Contents

To my dear wife Edna, who is now in the presence of her Lord whom she loved dearly. My God-given, faithful companion in our labors together for our blessed Lord.

Introduction

Great prominence is given in the Word of God to the earthly life of our Lord Jesus Christ. The four Gospels, which are the record of His earthly life, contain eighty-nine chapters out of the two hundred and sixty chapters in the New Testament. The fact that His life is set forth so prominently in the Scriptures is sufficient reason to believe that God would have every believer meditate upon this matchless life. The Holy Spirit will teach us much needed truth by a prayerful consideration of the life of our Lord.

Dr. Charles H. Spurgeon wrote, "We may be certain that whatever God has made prominent in His Word, He intended to be conspicuous in our lives." God has made very prominent in His Word the wonderful earthly life of our Lord, and has thus set forth His life as the example for us.

Dr. F. B. Meyer, commenting on I Peter 2:21, wrote, "It becomes us to mark well those footprints."

The Word of God is clear in its call for us to meditate upon this life in order that our lives should be patterned like it. "For consider him that endured such contradiction of sinners against himself, lest ye be wearied and faint in your minds" (Hebrews 12:3). "He that saith he abideth in him ought himself also so to walk, even as he walked" (I John 2:6).

The Lord Jesus Christ declared, "For I have given

you an example, that ye should do as I have done to you" (John 13:15).

The life which our Lord Jesus Christ lived in complete dependence upon His Father is the life of which we write. It becomes a pattern for a life of similar dependence which each believer should live, completely dependent upon the Son of God. We see this truth expressed in John 6:57, "As the living Father hath sent me, and I live by the Father: so he that eateth me, even he shall live by me."

The purpose, of course, for these meditations upon the life of Christ is that we may become like Christ in our daily living.

> By looking to Jesus,
> Like Him thou shalt be;
> Thy friends in thy conduct,
> His likeness will see.

The transforming of our lives into the image of Christ is performed by the Holy Spirit and not by self-effort.

As we behold the glory of our Lord Jesus Christ in the Word of God, the Holy Spirit within does His work of changing us into the image of Christ. "But we all, with open face beholding as in a glass the glory of the Lord, are changed into the same image from glory to glory, even as by the Spirit of the Lord" (II Cor. 3:18). The measure, therefore, in which the Holy Spirit is able to make the believer like Christ is dependent upon the believer earnestly beholding the glory of Christ in the Word of God.

The meditations in the life of Christ which follow have been a source of constant blessing to the writer over many years, and have satisfied a deep heart hunger to know Christ, and to be like Him. May God by His grace and mercy cause us all to hunger and thirst for Christ and to be abundantly satisfied with a deeper, transforming revelation of Christ in the Word.

Newton C. Conant

Chapter 1

BEHOLD HIM IN PRAYER

The prayer life of our Lord is deeply instructive and should become a pattern for the prayer life of every believer who would be like Christ. There are two basic thoughts relative to His life of prayer. First, *He devoted much time to prayer.* And second, *the events of His active life grew out of prayer;* that is, these events came to pass because of the prayer which preceded them.

I. The Lord Jesus Christ Devoted Much Time to Prayer.

"And it came to pass in those days, that he went out into a mountain to pray, and continued all night in prayer to God" (Luke 6:12).

Prayer was most costly to the Lord Jesus Christ in both time and energy. Outside of the actual suffering of the cross, the experience of prayer was perhaps His most costly experience. For instance, witness the sufferings of our Saviour in the prayer struggle in Gethsemane. Can prayer be so costly to Christ and yet be so cheap to us, His professed followers?

Much of the believer's time in prayer should be taken up with necessary heart-searching. We need time to allow God to search our motives and to reveal to us any evil way in which we may be walking. It is so easy for us to go astray from God, and we need daily heart-searching and cleansing to restore us. However, this was not so with our Lord Jesus Christ who knew no sin and who did no sin. Why then did our Lord find it so necessary to spend so much time alone in prayer with His Father? May we suggest at least five reasons:

1. The need of such fellowship with His Father which only long periods of time could satisfy.

2. The need to learn complete dependence upon the Father and thus to place all things in the Father's hands.

3. The need to replenish strength for His daily ministry in combat with the powers of darkness.

4. The need to get the very words from the Father which He should later speak that day.

5. The need for further light and instruction in God's will.

Are not these valid reasons for us also to spend much time daily in quietness and meditation in the presence of the Lord?

A. The Lord Jesus Christ Made Time for Prayer.

"And when he had sent the multitudes away, he went up into a mountain apart to pray; and when the evening was come, he was there alone" (Matthew 14:23).

When it was time for prayer it was more important to Jesus that He keep this appointment than it was to preach to throngs of people. He sent the throngs away or withdrew from them in order to make time for private prayer. "But so much the more went there a fame abroad of him: and great multitudes came together to hear, and to be healed by him of their infirmities. And he withdrew himself into the wilderness, and prayed" (Luke 5:15,16).

Prayer was, to Him at this time, more important than the healing ministry. He left off healing to pray. He often withdrew from the work He loved in order to be alone with the Father in prayer. Yes, He retired even from seasons of great blessing in order to seek the guidance and fellowship of His Father in prayer (Mark 1:32-35).

The believer must also learn to set definite times for prayer and devotion to the Lord, and by faith keep these times as sacred unto the Lord. We must so recognize the supreme importance of prayer as to give it proper precedence over all lesser, though seemingly important, matters. Men who have been greatly used of God have been men who set definite times for prayer which they kept diligently. Daniel, even when threatened by death if he did so, still kept his regular prayer times. "Now when Daniel knew that the writing was signed [a decree to cast to the lions all who called upon God], he went into his house; and his windows being open in his chamber toward Jerusalem, he kneeled upon his knees three times a day, and prayed, and gave thanks before his God, as he did aforetime" (Daniel 6:10).

All believers must learn from our Lord and from the example of men greatly used of God, that they must not be haphazard and careless in their prayer lives, hoping to find time to fit prayer in somewhere, somehow. This is the pathway of spiritual failure and defeat. Times for prayer must be set and must be observed faithfully if we are to follow the example of our Lord. These prayer times will become increasingly precious and will be looked forward to with great expectation, and will result in times of great blessing in the presence of the Lord.

B. His Favorite Time for Prayer Was the Morning.

"The Lord God hath given me the tongue of the learned, that I should know how to speak a word in season to him that is weary: he wakeneth morning by morning, he wakeneth mine ear to hear as the learned" (Isaiah 50:4).

Although the Lord Jesus Christ prayed as each need arose, yet the morning was His favorite time for prayer.

Morning by morning the Father is seen as awakening His Son from the slumber of the night in order to instruct Him. God spoke to Him directly and also through the written Word of God. The Lord of glory manifested in the flesh was meditating in the same Old Testament scriptures which we have. Each new day the Father confided in His dear Son.

How important it is for each child of God to allow the Lord to reach his heart the first thing each morning, before any competitor is introduced into the heart. Why should we set up opposition in our hearts to the Word of God and to the Holy Spirit? If we should read the newspaper or listen to the radio first each morning, we would most likely introduce into our hearts thoughts which would dim or be in conflict with the voice of God. How wonderful to let the Lord reach us first each morning, even before we speak to our loved ones.

An orchestra does not tune up its instruments

after the concert is over. The wise child of God meets the Lord each morning before the burdens and trials of the day are faced. Then when difficulties come, the believer faces them with spiritual strength and with the wisdom of God. It is well to meet the Lord also at the close of the day. But how foolish to face all of the day's burdens without first having met the Lord and allowed Him to refresh and strengthen us. Each morning our Saviour received instructions for that day. The Lord God each morning gave Him the tongue of the learned (Isaiah 50:4). No wonder the people were amazed at what gracious words proceeded from His mouth (Luke 4:22).

There is much in this to instruct us. No one must undertake to be a teacher for God who has not first been taught by God, and the best time to be taught is each morning. The Lord Jesus knew how to speak a word in season to him that was weary, because He was taught of God. He stated that the very words He spoke were words He received from His Father. "The words that I speak unto you I speak not of myself" (John 14:10). "I do nothing of myself; but as my Father hath taught me, I speak these things" (John 8:28). "For I have not spoken of myself; but the Father which sent me, he gave me a commandment, what I should say, and what I should speak" (John 12:49). No wonder that when He taught in the synagogue the people were astonished and inquired, "Whence hath this man this wisdom?" (Matthew 13:54). The Lord Jesus Christ knew how to succor with words because He received these comforting words from His Father each morning.

Words given by God have the power to lift up, to comfort, and to encourage the downtrodden. There is a divine medicine in the words He gives. It is so important in ministering to a weary people to have words from God. How often does it happen that the very message received from God in the early morning devotions will be the words some weary pilgrim will need that very day to encourage him. "If the root be holy, so are the branches" (Romans 11:16). If the root of every day be made holy in prayer, the hours that follow in that day will likewise be holy hours.

In answer to believing prayer, God will enable us to speak the words we should speak. We see this clearly illustrated when the apostles in the early church were ordered, under severe threats by the Sanhedrin, "not to speak at all nor teach in the name of Jesus." The church went to prayer. The prayer was, "And now, Lord, behold their threatenings: and grant unto thy servants, that with all boldness they may speak thy word. . . ." In response, "the place was shaken where they were assembled together; and they were all filled with the Holy Ghost, and they spake the word of God with boldness" (Acts 4:29, 31).

The Apostle Paul constantly asked prayer for his lips. "[Pray] for me, that utterance may be given unto me, that I may open my mouth boldly, to make known the mystery of the gospel" (Ephesians 6:19).

The Holy Spirit desires to give us words which apply to our particular situation or need. The Lord Jesus Christ "healed the broken-hearted" and bound up wounds with words. He raised up with words those who were exhausted with sin and suffering. Ability to do this is one of God's best gifts, which we should earnestly covet. What a ministry to encourage others in the Lord, to give strength to the tempted, comfort to those who mourn, and to lead the defeated into victory.

If the believer does not regularly meet the Lord over His Word each morning, he will have nothing to give to the needy of earth. How tragic it is to have someone before you with a tremendous need, and then to realize the best you are offering is mere human wisdom because of neglect to previously wait upon God. God taught me this lesson years ago in such a manner that I shall never forget it. It seemed I was being prompted by the Holy Spirit, after my Bible reading, to retire for morning prayer and to open myself to all that God had to say to me. I foolishly and continually put off getting on my knees before the Lord, using the excuse that I would wait for the morning mail and perhaps find new material in the mail for prayer. The Holy Spirit gently urged me to prayer, but I waited too long. There was a knock on the door but it was not the mailman. A needy brother in Christ came to talk over with me a deep problem in his life, seeking counsel and help. I have never forgotten the awfulness of the realization that I had nothing to offer him, except my human wisdom. I believe God would have given me the very message this brother needed if I had heeded the call of the Holy Spirit and given myself to prayer before he arrived. I failed him because I first failed God.

Words have a great comforting and healing power if they are words received from God and spoken in the power of the Holy Spirit. It is said of the Lord Jesus that grace was poured into His lips (Psalm 45:2). There must be time given to God for Him to pour grace into our lips or gracious words will never

come forth from us. There is no better time to meet
the Lord and receive these gracious words from Him
than each morning. The Lord Jesus Christ spoke
constantly as one instructed in the things of God,
and therefore He was enabled to give a word of good
cheer from God. He knew how to sustain with
words. We are living in a weary, worn world—and
true believers in the Lord Jesus Christ are not ex-
empt from weariness and strain. God wants us to
reach these who are weary of earth, and God brings
these weary ones across our pathway that we may
cheer them with words which we have previously
received from Him. The Lord Jesus came forth from
the secret communing with His Father refreshed and
ready. "Never man spake like this man" (John
7:46).

Years ago, an elderly Christian woman told the
writer of the great encouragement she had received
because of just a word from her pastor, who was Dr.
G. Campbell Morgan. This woman came out to prayer meeting very tired after a day of standing on her
feet behind the counter in the bookstore where she
was employed. Dr. Morgan, before the meeting began, saw her—and no doubt took into his heart her
tired condition. He came down from the pulpit and
stood by her pew and tenderly asked her just a one-
word question: "Tired?" This woman told me how
such a blessing and such a peace came into her heart,
just to know that he was concerned that she was
tired. She felt the healing quality of a word spoken
in the power of the Lord by one who was concerned. This experience was so uplifting to her that
she felt led to relate it to many others.

The Word of God contains a very helpful picture
of the believer's hidden life. It is likened to the roots

of a tree going down into the waters, providing strength and fruitfulness for the tree. "For he shall be as a tree planted by the waters, and that spreadeth out her roots by the river" (Jeremiah 17:8). The roots are the hidden life of the tree. This part of the tree which cannot be seen supports and provides the life for the visible part of the tree. The hidden roots search for the water and, finding it, produce life and fruit for the tree. If the roots are in the water the tree will still be bearing fruit, and the leaf will remain green, even in time of scorching heat. So it is with the believer. It is not the severity of the trial which causes us to be fruitless. No matter how intense the heat becomes, if our roots are in the water the tree will still be bearing fruit. Some of God's dear saints have, in times of most difficult trial, borne the choicest fruit.

Every tree has a proper proportion of roots to branches. The branches speak of Christian activity. What would happen should there be a tree that was all branches and no roots? The misshapen thing would dry up and collapse. But even before drying up and collapsing it would undoubtedly blow over with the first gust of wind, because it had nothing supporting it. Is not this the reason why many Christians are living fruitless and defeated lives, and seem to be in a state of spiritual collapse? They are all branches of activity and have no hidden root-life of refreshing in the presence of their Lord.

Because of the dulling experiences of life we all need a daily renewing by our God (II Corinthians 4:16). Our ministry will only be as fresh and new as our spiritual life is made fresh and new in the presence of the Lord (Acts 3:19). And may I again stress that, following the example of the Lord Jesus

Christ, the best time to meet the Lord is the first thing each morning.

II. Events in the Life of the Lord Jesus Christ Grew out of Prayer Which Preceded These Events.

This is a most fascinating and rewarding meditation: to see how many major events in the life and ministry of Christ were preceded by prayer and brought to pass by prayer.

A. He Prayed Before the Anointing With the Holy Spirit at His Baptism.

"Now when all the people were baptized, it came to pass that Jesus also being baptized, and praying . . ." (Luke 3:21).

He was not praying idly. What followed gives us the clue to His prayer. In answer to His prayer, the heavens opened and the Holy Ghost descended in a bodily shape like a dove upon Him, and a voice came from heaven which said, "Thou art my beloved Son; in thee I am well pleased" (Luke 3:22). His prayer caused the heavens to part and the Holy Spirit to be manifested visibly, and God's voice certified the Lord Jesus Christ as His Son. This was the sign to John the Baptist that Jesus was the very Christ (John 1:32–34).

It is interesting to note that three times God's voice was heard from heaven, by which the Father bore witness to His Son. Each time the voice was heard while He was praying, or very soon thereafter (Luke 9:28–35; John 12:27,28).

B. He Prayed to Get Direction for His Ministry.

The Lord Jesus Christ had spent a very busy day of ministry. He had gone to the synagogue and taught (Mark 1:21). While in the synagogue He delivered a man from an unclean spirit. After leaving, He healed Peter's wife's mother of her fever. The day was now drawing to a close. And as the sun was setting "they brought unto him all that were diseased, and them that were possessed with demons . . . . He healed many that were sick of divers diseases and cast out many demons" (Mark 1:32–34). A large crowd of people was there, we are told: "And all the city was gathered together at the door" (vs. 33). The Lord Jesus Christ apparently had little sleep that night because "in the morning, rising up a great while before day, he went out, and departed into a solitary place, and there prayed" (Mark 1:35).

Sometimes it is more important to seek the will of God in prayer than to have our necessary sleep. The question before Him was this: should He continue His ministry here or move on in the will of God to other towns? He did not presume to know the will of the Father for the place of His ministry. He did not judge by externals alone. The place where He was now ministering was such a fruitful field that it would seem wise to remain a little longer. However, when He learned the will of His Father He left this miracle work and moved on.

We should follow this example of our Lord and, like Philip (Acts 8:26,27), be so schooled to obedience to the will of God that we are willing to leave a place where God has been abundantly blessing and step out into the unknown alone with Him.

Human wisdom was not long in coming from

Peter and the other disciples. They seemed to say, "Where have You been? All men seek Thee." Well-meaning dear friends may assume to know the will of God for us, but their advice is to be rejected in the light of what we learn from God Himself while alone in prayer.

The place of ministry was revealed to the Lord Jesus Christ by God in prayer, and He quickly fit into the Father's program for Him with these words, "Let us go into the next towns, that I may preach there also: for therefore came I forth" (Mark 1:38).

How necessary it is for the Christian to be cast utterly upon God so as to allow Him to choose the very place of his ministry. How wonderful to let the choice be in God's hands. Just as the Son of God was not permitted to choose the place of His ministry, neither were the apostles allowed to do so. Paul and Silas were forbidden of the Holy Ghost to preach the word in the province of Asia, and as "they assayed to go into Bithynia, the Spirit suffered them not," but after they saw in a vision a man of Macedonia appealing for help, they assuredly gathered that the Lord had called them to preach the gospel in Macedonia (Acts 16:6–10).

Looking back over nearly fifty years of serving the Lord, the writer cannot help but praise God for His faithfulness in directing him to the very places of God's choice. How necessary this is for those who minister. It is absolutely impossible for any believer to know unaided by God the best place for him to minister. Who but God knows all the events past and future? Who but God knows where we will best fit into His plans? Who but God knows the complete plans for each generation in this world? How safe therefore and how necessary to leave the place of our ministry in *His* hands. Only in this way can God be glorified and our fullest possibilities for fruitfulness be realized.

C. He Prayed When Fame Threatened.

"But so much the more went there a fame abroad of him: and great multitudes came together . . . . And he withdrew himself into the wilderness, and prayed" (Luke 5:15,16).

When praise and honor come from men there is a special need for prayer and meditation in the presence of the Lord. Often praise comes from shallow hearts, and from those who offer it for some selfish advantage. If we foolishly accept this praise and feed upon it, serious spiritual damage will result. In such times as these there is often severe temptation to self-exultation and independence. If yielded to, this results in the believer becoming useless to God, and he must be chastened to bring him back again to lowliness and dependency. It becomes very difficult for a Christian to maintain a spirit of dependence and lowliness in times of great spiritual and material blessing. Nor do we usually feel a great need to pray during such times. And accompanying a *spirit* of independence there is a severe temptation to go beyond the will of God in some *act* of self-expression.

Uzziah, the king of Judah, was a man greatly used of God. His record of achievements were many and notable. The secret of his life up to this point is found in II Chronicles 26:5, "As long as he sought the Lord, God made him to prosper." However, during this time of great prosperity his heart was lifted up to his own destruction. He foolishly sought to assume the right of the priest and offered incense upon the altar—contrary to the will of God and despite the urgent pleading of Azariah and eighty other priests. His previous good record could not now be pleaded in his defense. He was stricken with leprosy, and lived and died in a cottage apart (II Chronicles 26:16–21). How different it would have been for Uzziah if he had retired for prayer and heart-searching in the presence of the Lord in the time when he was at the peak of his prosperity and blessing.

So it would be well for all of us to withdraw for prayer when great spiritual or material blessing seems to threaten us with pride. The man who led the writer to Christ said frequently, "My, how God will use anyone who will be careful to give God all the glory." Failure to give God the glory will lead to walking in the self-life with its inevitable barrenness.

What a lesson there is for us in the life of our Lord. He felt a special need when fame threatened; God help us to see a similar need in our own lives. This dangerous situation of prosperity may be completely solved in the presence of the Lord, and we can leave the place of prayer humbled and cleansed both from any reliance upon ourselves and from feeding upon the praises of men. Let us all take note of the heart-searching question uttered by our Lord in John 5:44: "How can ye believe, which receive honor one of another and seek not the honor that cometh from God only?"

D. He Prayed When the Thoughtless Would Make Him King.

"When Jesus therefore perceived that they would

come and take him by force, to make him a king, he departed again into a mountain himself alone" (John 6:15).

After the miracle of the loaves and fishes the thoughtless multitude desired to make Jesus king. There was no idea of surrender to Him as the Son of God however. They were materialistic self-seekers. Here perhaps, they may have thought, is a man who through His miracles will keep us supplied with the necessities of life. At this point Christ retired for prayer and meditation. He returned from prayer with this stinging rebuke to them, "Verily, verily, I say unto you, Ye seek me, not because ye saw the miracles, but because ye did eat of the loaves, and were filled. Labor not for the meat which perisheth, but for that meat which endureth unto everlasting life, which the Son of man shall give unto you: for him hath God the Father sealed" (John 6:26,27).

Prayer enabled Him to see very clearly the motives of those who would exalt Him and advance Him for selfish reasons which were not in the will of God. Prayer will likewise enable us to have good spiritual perception, and in prayer God will grant us wisdom to see through the fleshly schemes of people who would favor us for their own selfish interests.

E. He Prayed Before the Choosing of the Twelve Apostles.

"And it came to pass in those days, that he went out into a mountain to pray, and continued all night in prayer to God. And when it was day, he called unto him his disciples: and of them he chose twelve, whom also he named apostles" (Luke 6:12,13).

The burden of the night's devotion, a solemn prolonged communion, was preparation for the appointment of the twelve apostles. How very important that the very ones chosen by God should be revealed to Christ. How necessary that John and Peter be chosen and even Judas. The apostles were to write much of the New Testament, and their teachings were to become the foundation of the church. Yes, we "are built upon the foundation of the apostles and prophets, Jesus Christ himself being the chief corner stone" (Ephesians 2:20).

Why an all-night prayer session? All the names of the apostles could have been revealed to Christ in an instant of time. A very important lesson is to be learned. The important matter in prayer is not always the receiving of a quick answer. Prayer is also to teach us absolute dependence upon God and the need of deeper communion with Him. Our Lord is not only to receive the answer to His prayer, but also to realize once more the great value of dependence and communion.

The Lord Jesus Christ realized He must not make the choice of the twelve dependent upon His own wisdom. He is not to judge by outward appearances nor to have any personal preferences.

How wonderful it would be and how different our churches would be if officers were selected after a night of prayer. What blessing would come to churches if they truly depended upon the Lord Jesus Christ, and in communion with Him allowed Him to make known the names of those whom He has chosen. So often there is a choice of officers and leaders on a fleshly basis (and the only result of the flesh is corruption). Hasty selection of officers on the basis of personal preference or other considerations, without seeking God's clear will, results in terrible hindrance to the work of God.

The church at Antioch recognized the need of waiting upon God for the selection of those who were to lead in the missionary outreach of that testimony. "As they ministered to the Lord, and fasted, the Holy Ghost said, Separate me Barnabas and Saul for the work whereunto I have called them" (Acts 13:2).

When the Lord laid His hand upon me recently and indicated that I was to leave the church I had been privileged to pastor for nearly thirty-nine years, the deacons of the church took two separate afternoons for prayer at Keswick Grove, New Jersey, asking God to burden the man of His choice and to compel him to come as the new pastor. Prayer was made in much assurance that God had His man ready and would make him known. In a marvelous way God burdened the man of His choice and led him to assume the pastorate. We were all amazed, and glorified God. When God's man finds God's place in answer to prayer, great blessing is sure to result.

F. He Prayed Before Peter's Great Confession.

The Lord Jesus Christ was alone praying. When He came from the presence of God to the disciples, a question directed to them was upon His lips: "Whom say the people that I am?" (Luke 9:18). Impressions received in prayer are so important. When we come fresh from the presence of God we have the mind of God. It seems evident that the great subject of the prayer of Christ in the presence of God was the need that the spiritual eyes of the apostles should be opened by a revelation to them of who He is. So the Lord Jesus Christ prayed for them before He questioned them concerning His Person. In Matthew 16:14–16 we read the outcome: "They said, Some say that thou art John the Baptist: some, Elias; and others, Jeremias, or one of the prophets. He saith unto them, But whom say ye that I am? And Simon Peter answered and said, Thou art the Christ, the Son of the living God." This was the correct answer.

How did Peter learn this? It was not by human wisdom but by divine revelation: "And Jesus answered and said unto him, Blessed art thou, Simon Bar-jona: for flesh and blood hath not revealed it unto thee, but my Father which is in heaven" (Matthew 16:17). God the Father had revealed to Peter the truth concerning the Person of Christ. This revelation came in answer to the prayer of Christ which preceded it.

God is still revealing who Jesus is in answer to prayer. "Wherefore I also, after I heard of your faith in the Lord Jesus, and love unto all the saints, cease not to give thanks for you, making mention of you in my prayers; that the God of our Lord Jesus Christ, the Father of glory, may give unto you the spirit of wisdom and revelation in the knowledge of him" (Ephesians 1:15–17).

It is so very important to the personal life and fruitfulness of the believer that he should know who Jesus is. The believer should know that Jesus is the Son of God, with all authority and with all power. He should know Him as He is and should reckon constantly upon Him. This understanding will come to us in answer to prayer, and to others also in answer to our prayers. Defeated Christians simply need to know who Jesus is and to rest upon His power and sufficiency. This revelation comes in answer to prayer.

G. He Prayed Before His Transfiguration.

"And it came to pass about an eight days after these sayings, he took Peter and John and James, and went up into a mountain to pray. And as he prayed, the fashion of his countenance was altered, and his raiment was white and glistering" (Luke 9:28,29).

His face shone far beyond the glow on the face of Moses when Moses was with the Lord on Mt. Sinai (Exodus 34:29). It was the restoration temporarily of the glory which He had with the Father before the world was (John 17:5). Peter wrote, describing the scene, "We were eyewitnesses of his majesty" (II Peter 1:16). John spoke of it in these words, "We beheld his glory, the glory as of the only begotten of the Father" (John 1:14). This whole glorious scene came as the consequence of His prayer.

It was a time of growing enmity toward Christ, a token of His final rejection and crucifixion. The cross loomed up just ahead, and He knew it. Now there appeared with Him in glory Moses and Elijah, and they talked with Him concerning His decease which He should accomplish in Jerusalem. How wonderful it must have been for Christ to have Moses and Elijah talk with Him about His coming death on the cross. How it must have confirmed to Him that He was in God's will, and how it must have encouraged Him in this crucial hour. How concerned heaven was with His coming cross.

His prayer on the mount may seem to have been

unfinished, because as He was praying the transfiguration took place. But the whole scene was an answer to His prayer and resulted from it.

As with Him, so with us. Our Lord in heaven cares for us and is greatly concerned as daily we take up our cross and follow Him (Luke 9:23). God is the God of all encouragement (II Corinthians 1:1–5). Encouragement will come to us as we lay the matter before Him in prayer. He will show us the necessity of our cross and give great courage to bear it. Earth hath no sorrow which heaven cannot heal.

H. He Prayed Before He Raised Lazarus From the Dead.

"Then they took away the stone from the place where the dead was laid. And Jesus lifted up his eyes, and said, Father, I thank thee that thou hast heard me. And I knew that thou hearest me always: but because of the people which stand by I said it, that they may believe that thou hast sent me" (John 11:41,42).

In prayer some four days earlier the Lord Jesus Christ had dealt with the entire situation of the illness and death of Lazarus, and thus the mind of God was clear to Him what He was to do. He knew after this prayer that He would call forth Lazarus from the dead, and thus display the truth that He is the resurrection and the life (John 11:25).

He said, "Father, I thank thee that thou hast heard me" (John 11:41). Our Lord was now giving thanks in advance for an answer to the prayer previously offered. "And when he had thus spoken, he cried with a loud voice, Lazarus, come forth. And he that was dead came forth" (John 11:43,44). The resurrection of Lazarus was the answer to our Lord's prayer which preceded it. How wonderful to face our overwhelming problems with the assurance that God has previously heard our prayer concerning these problems and is about to work in miracle power.

I. He Prayed Before Foretelling Peter's Fall and Restoration.

"And the Lord said, Simon, Simon, behold, Satan hath desired to have you, that he may sift you as wheat: but I have prayed for thee, that thy faith fail not: and when thou art converted, strengthen thy brethren" (Luke 22:31, 32).

The Lord Jesus Christ knew that the proud, boastful tendencies in Peter's life could only produce the inevitable fall. A proud, boastful, self-sufficient Christian is easy prey for Satan. Pride and self-sufficiency will sooner or later lead to denials of the faith and of the Lord.

Before Peter's fall the Lord Jesus Christ prayed that Peter's faith would not fail. Our Lord won the victory in prayer for Peter before the test even took place. So sure was the Lord Jesus Christ that Peter would be restored that He gave Peter the commission to strengthen the brethren after his restoration. The Satanic test came and Peter denied his Lord three times. However, when Peter's conscience was awakened to the enormity of his denials, he did not turn back from the faith but went out and in repentance wept bitterly. The Lord later gave him gracious words of restoration and recommission (John 21:15–17).

How wonderfully Peter later uses this dreadful experience to strengthen his brethren. Peter instructs the Christian on the basis of his experience, "Be sober, be vigilant; because your adversary the devil, as a roaring lion, walketh about, seeking whom he may devour: whom resist stedfast in the faith, knowing that the same afflictions are accomplished in your brethren that are in the world" (I Peter 5:8,9).

The Christian has a real ministry in prayer for those who have failed under Satanic attack. We need to pray that the faith of these Christians will not fail, but that they will be restored and used to strengthen other brethren. It is our duty to ask God to open our eyes to see our brethren who are under attack, to pray earnestly for them, and to believe God for their restoration and their further usefulness.

J. He Prayed Before His Crucifixion.

The Lord Jesus Christ learned anew in Gethsemane what He had known all along, that there would be no deliverance from the cross, but that there would be deliverance out of death. He learned a deeper meaning of obedience by the things which He suffered.

The words which describe Gethsemane are very suggestive of the intense suffering He endured as He prayed. "Sorrowful and very heavy" (Matthew 26:37); "My soul is exceeding sorrowful, even unto death" (vs. 38); "He . . . fell on his face" (vs. 39); "He . . . began to be sore amazed" (Mark 14:33); "Being in an agony he prayed more earnestly: and his sweat was as it were great drops of blood falling down to the ground" (Luke 22:44).

Christ could have asked for more than twelve legions of angels to be at His side to deliver Him, but how then would the prophecies be fulfilled? He saw His pathway clearly marked out in the Word of God. "Thinkest thou that I cannot now pray to my Father, and he shall presently give me more than twelve legions of angels? But how then shall the scriptures be fulfilled, that thus it must be?" (Matthew 26:53,54). He saw the cup now as from the Father's hand and calmly declared, "The cup which my Father hath given me, shall I not drink it?" (John 18:11). The battle was over, the victory won in prayer, and now He resolutely faced the cross. He prayed Himself to the cross.

We learn to face life's deepest experiences in the will of God by submissive prayer with the same words upon our lips which He uttered, "The cup which my Father hath given me, shall I not drink it?" (John 18:11).

K. He Prayed While On the Cross.

"Father, forgive them; for they know not what they do" (Luke 23:34).

The Lord Jesus Christ was in terrible physical condition at this time. He was so marred that His appearance was not that of a man (Isaiah 52:14). This condition was caused by the bloody sweat in Gethsemane and the scourging in Pilate's hall. Besides that, His bones were out of joint; His tongue was cleaving to His mouth in extreme thirst; His hands and His feet were pierced with nails; His body torn by convulsions. Yet He is not concerned at this time over His own wounds but about the desperate need of the offenders. He is forgetful of Himself and of His own physical needs in the presence of the spiritual needs of others.

His life was one hundred percent consistent with His teaching. He had taught, "Love your enemies, bless them that curse you, do good to them that hate you, and pray for them which despitefully use you, and persecute you" (Matthew 5:44).

He prayed with the calmness of one cast upon God. "I was cast upon thee" (Psalm 22:10). What a contrast to His calmness was the tumult about the cross where the air was filled with blasphemies and curses and the mockery of those who were clamoring for His death.

He prayed not that they might be consumed or destroyed, but that they might be forgiven. This was their desperate need—forgiveness. It was the longing passion of His heart which He expressed, not a sentimental saying just to awaken sympathy. The Lord Jesus Christ would cover the heads of His murderers with the shield of His love. He would shelter them from the wrath of God. He prayed the best for those who wished the worst for Him.

The very blood He was then shedding was the only basis of their forgiveness. "For this is my blood of the new testament, which is shed for many for the remission of sins" (Matthew 26:28).

He pleaded as an attorney does, pointing out even the least things which may be in their favor: "For they know not what they do." Do we ever recall anything which may be in the favor of those who have injured us? It was true they did not know. Paul wrote: "For had they known it, they would not have crucified the Lord of glory" (I Corinthians 2:8); and Peter said, "I know that through ignorance

ye did it" (Acts 3:17). However, it was *guilty* ignorance, and they *needed* forgiveness or He would not
have earnestly prayed for their forgiveness. Peter
tells us, "Him, being delivered by the determinate
counsel and foreknowledge of God, ye have taken,
and by wicked hands have crucified and slain" (Acts
2:23). Isaiah tells us, "He bare the sin of many, and
made intercession for the transgressors" (Isaiah
53:12).

It may be asked, Was this prayer for their forgiveness answered? The thief crucified on a cross near to
Christ may have been greatly helped by this prayer
for forgiveness of the offenders. This prayer could
have been a great encouragement to him to turn to
the Lord Jesus Christ and ask to be remembered
when He would come into His kingdom—and what
wonderful words implying forgiveness were spoken
to him: "Verily I say unto thee, Today shalt thou be
with me in paradise" (Luke 23:43).

There is evidence of the working of God upon the
centurion's heart and others when they exclaimed,
"Certainly this was a righteous man" (Luke 23:47);
"Truly this was the Son of God" (Matthew 27:54).

Yes, those who did the actual crucifying received
forgiveness. And not only they but many others
also. Let us recall the words of Peter on the day of
Pentecost: "Ye men of Israel, hear these words:
Jesus of Nazareth . . . ye have taken, and by wicked
hands have crucified and slain . . . . Therefore let all
the house of Israel know assuredly, that God hath
made that same Jesus, whom ye have crucified, both
Lord and Christ." Yes, the whole nation was respon-
sible; and these men recognized their collective guilt.
"Now when they heard this, they were pricked in
their heart, and said unto Peter and to the rest of

the apostles, Men and brethren, what shall we do? Then Peter said unto them, Repent, and be baptized every one of you in the name of Jesus Christ for the remission of sins, and ye shall receive the gift of the Holy Ghost . . . . Then they that gladly received his word were baptized; and the same day there were added unto them about three thousand souls" (Acts 2:22–41). Isn't it wonderful to see this manifestation of the grace of God? These repentant men—some of whom may have been in that murderous mob about the cross—were saved on the day of Pentecost and became part of the first church.

Peter's second sermon is likewise addressed to those who were guilty of the crucifixion of the Lord Jesus Christ. "The God of Abraham, and of Isaac, and of Jacob, the God of our fathers, hath glorified his Son Jesus; whom ye delivered up, and denied him in the presence of Pilate, when he was determined to let him go. But ye denied the Holy One and the Just, and desired a murderer to be granted unto you; and killed the Prince of life, whom God hath raised from the dead; whereof we are witnesses . . . . Howbeit many of them which heard the word believed; and the number of the men was about five thousand" (Acts 3:13–15, 4:4.) Here again is another definite answer to the prayer of the Lord Jesus Christ from His cross.

Another remarkable statement was made in Acts 6:7: "A great company of the priests were obedient to the faith." The Word of God is very clear as to the former hostility of these priests, from the high priest on down: "Now the chief priests, and elders, and all the council sought false witness against Jesus to put him to death" (Matthew 26:59). "The chief priests and elders persuaded the multitude that they should ask [for] Barabbas, and destroy Jesus" (Matthew 27:20). How wonderful therefore that a great company of these priests should be saved.

Yes, this prayer of Christ on the cross for the forgiveness of those who crucified Him was answered. Many of those who cried out "Crucify him, crucify him" were wonderfully saved, and are now with the Lord in glory. Their salvation was the result of His prayer on the cross.

L. He Prayed Before the Coming of the Holy Spirit at Pentecost.

The coming of the Holy Spirit on the day of Pentecost to the believers assembled in the upper room was in answer to Jesus' prayer to the Father. He told His disciples who were sorrowing over His statement that He was about to leave them, "And I will pray the Father, and he shall give you another Comforter, that he may abide with you forever; even the Spirit of truth; whom the world cannot receive, because it seeth him not, neither knoweth him: but ye know him; for he dwelleth with you, and shall be in you" (John 14:16,17).

As our great High Priest, the Lord Jesus Christ still prays. "Wherefore he is able also to save them to the uttermost that come unto God by him, seeing he ever liveth to make intercession for them" (Hebrews 7:25). In answer to His present prayer in the glory, God's people are sustained and kept through their earthly pilgrimage. The prayer of intercession recorded in John 17 reveals a little of the great heart of love which Christ has for His own as He pleads with the Father on behalf of "them which thou hast given me" (John 17:9). And His intercession for His own will continue until all the redeemed are safe in His presence, beholding His glory (John 17:24).

This meditation upon the prayer life of our Lord should cause each believer to cry to God for constant cleansing from the sin of prayerlessness. Beholding Jesus Christ, each disciple of His should be convinced of the absolute necessity of giving prayer the primary place in his life. For only then will we experience that life of God-planned fruitfulness and blessing which our Saviour desires for each one He has redeemed by His blood.

> My God! is any hour so sweet,
>> From blush of morn to evening star,
> As that which calls me to Thy feet,
>> The hour of prayer?

—Charlotte Elliott

Chapter 2

BEHOLD HIM USING THE WORD OF GOD

It is most helpful and instructive for a Christian to meditate on the attitude of our Lord Jesus Christ toward the Scriptures. The believer will discover what a prominent place the Scriptures had in the life of our Lord. The Scriptures must have a place of primary importance in our lives too, if we are to follow His example. So let us consider what the Word of God meant to Him.

I. The Lord Jesus Christ Believed the Old Testament Scriptures.

He declared them to be the Word of God which could not be broken or annulled. "The scripture cannot be broken" (John 10:35). He stated that all of the law would be fulfilled. "For verily I say unto you, Till heaven and earth pass, one jot or one tittle shall in no wise pass from the law, till all be fulfilled" (Matthew 5:18).

The character of the witness cannot but affect the weight of His testimony. When we consider that the Lord Jesus Christ is the Son of the living God, "in whom are hid all the treasures of wisdom and knowledge" (Colossians 2:3), then what weight should be given to His testimony concerning the

Scriptures. If for no other reason, we can fully believe the Old Testament on the authority of the Lord Jesus Christ.

II. The Lord Jesus Christ Believed the Much-Disputed Old Testament Miracles.

It is very difficult, if not impossible, for the natural man to accept the miraculous, because he cannot explain miracles on the basis of anything in his own experience. "The natural man receiveth not the things of the Spirit of God: for they are foolishness unto him: neither can he know them, because they are spiritually discerned" (I Corinthians 2:14). There are many miracles in the Old Testament which are ridiculed today by the unsaved. It is very significant that when the Lord Jesus Christ cited some of these miracles He not only stated His belief in them but also declared them to be illustrations of vital New Testament doctrines.

A. The Miracle of the Brazen Serpent.

"The people spake against God, and against Moses .... And the Lord sent fiery serpents among the people, and they bit the people; and much people of Israel died" (Numbers 21:5,6).

Upon their confession of sin, Moses prayed for them, and God prescribed a remedy: "Make thee a fiery serpent, and set it upon a pole: and it shall come to pass, that every one that is bitten, when he looketh upon it, shall live" (Numbers 21:8).

The Lord Jesus Christ stated that Moses *did* lift up the brazen serpent in the wilderness. As this was essential for the healing of the physically perishing Israelite, even so must He as our sin-bearer be lifted up on a cross for the salvation of the spiritually perishing world. "And as Moses lifted up the serpent in the wilderness, even so must the Son of man be lifted up: that whosoever believeth in him should not perish, but have eternal life. For God so loved the world, that he gave his only begotten Son, that whosoever believeth in him should not perish, but have everlasting life" (John 3:14–16).

Salvation is possible for the sinner only because the Lord Jesus Christ was lifted up on a cross as an offering for his sins. When the sinner, realizing his sinful and lost condition, looks to Christ in faith, he passes immediately from spiritual death to eternal life. When an Israelite who was bitten by the serpent looked at the uplifted brazen serpent, he was immediately healed of that which would have soon caused his physical death.

Would our Lord have used a myth or a lie upon which to base the truth of salvation made possible through His death on the cross?

B. The Miracle of Jonah and the Whale.

No miracle has been more ridiculed by the natural mind than the miracle of the preservation of Jonah in the whale's belly, and his subsequent deliverance from the whale—this miracle which took place in order to have Jonah preach the message of the Lord in Nineveh, the very duty from which he had previously fled (Jonah 1:1–3:2). Was this only a myth or fable? Our Lord Jesus Christ declared the Biblical record to be accurate history, and stated Jonah's experience was a type of His own resurrection. "For as Jonas was three days and three nights in the whale's belly; so shall the Son of man be three days and three nights in the heart of the earth" (Matthew 12:40). "For as Jonas was a sign to the Ninevites [after his deliverance from the whale], so shall the Son of man be to this generation" (Luke 11:30).

The Lord Jesus Christ, therefore, affirmed the Biblical record concerning Jonah and the whale. He stated that Jonah's miraculous deliverance is a type of His own resurrection. Our Lord was only three days and three nights in the tomb, and then He came forth in glorious resurrection power to be a sign to that generation, even as Jonah was a sign to the Ninevites after his deliverance from the whale's belly.

C. The Miracle of the Manna.

The Bible declares: "The children of Israel did eat manna forty years, until they came to a land inhabited; they did eat manna, until they came unto the borders of the land of Canaan" (Exodus 16:35).

This miracle is also much disputed and questioned by the natural mind. It seems so difficult to believe that God sent, morning by morning, for forty years, this food from heaven to sustain these people. The manna was "a small, round thing, as small as the hoar frost on the ground .... It was like coriander seed, white; and the taste of it was like wafers made with honey" (Exodus 16:14,31). He "rained down manna upon them to eat, and had given them of the corn of heaven. Man did eat angel's food" (Psalm 78:24,25).

In the sixth chapter of John, following the miracle of the loaves and fishes, our Lord gave a great message concerning Himself as the bread of life. He declared Himself to be the bread of God "which cometh down from heaven and giveth life unto the world" (John 6:33). "I am the bread of life: he that cometh to me shall never hunger; and he that believeth on me shall never thirst" (John 6:35). The Jews murmured when He said, "I am the bread which came down from heaven." Then He further declared, "Verily, verily, I say unto you, He that believeth on me hath everlasting life. I am that bread of life. Your fathers did eat manna in the wilderness, and are dead. This is the bread which cometh down from heaven, that a man may eat thereof, and not die" (John 6:47–50).

The Lord Jesus Christ certified to the genuineness of the miracle of the daily supply of manna. He said, "Your fathers did eat manna in the wilderness and are dead." He cited the miracle to show the contrast between the Israelites who ate manna in the wilderness and later died, and those who eat the Lord Jesus Christ, the true Bread from heaven, and as a result will never perish but have everlasting life.

D. The Record of Noah and the Ark.

This record perhaps, in the strictest sense, should not be called a miracle. It is, however, an account of God's miraculous provision in preserving Noah and his family and the living creatures from the judgment of the flood (Genesis 7–9). This story also has called forth much denunciation and ridicule.

Yet the Lord Jesus Christ declared the record of Noah and the ark to be true. He stated that there would be conditions on the earth just before His second coming similar to what existed before the flood. "But of that day and hour knoweth no man, no, not the angels of heaven, but my Father only. But as the days of Noe were, so shall also the coming of the Son of man be. For as in the days that were before the flood they were eating and drinking, marrying and giving in marriage, until the day that Noe entered into the ark, and knew not until the flood came, and took them all away; so shall also the coming of the Son of man be" (Matthew 24:36–39). The flood was sudden and unexpected; so shall the return of Christ be.

It is very clear that the Lord Jesus Christ believed the historicity of the story of Noah and the flood. He stated that the times of Noah were an accurate illustration of the very times which would prevail upon earth just before He would return.

How very significant that our Lord used these four miracles as illustrations of New Testament truths. If the miracles, therefore, are not true, then what about the doctrines which our Lord taught from these miracles and which these miracles illustrate?

These four vital doctrines of our faith would immediately be brought into question if these Old Testament miracles are not true:

1. The provision for salvation through the Cross.
2. The resurrection of the Lord Jesus Christ from the dead.
3. The ability of Christ to give the bread of eternal life.
4. The second coming of our Lord Jesus Christ.

A genuine believer in the Lord Jesus Christ has no further doubts concerning these miracles once he sees that his Lord declared them to be accurate history.

III. The Lord Jesus Christ Saw Himself Revealed in the Word of God.

He declared that the Scriptures spoke of Him: "Search the scriptures; for in them ye think ye have eternal life: and they are they which testify of me" (John 5:39).

He was saturated with the Word of God, and so became familiar with the many references in the Scriptures to Himself.

When He visited His native town of Nazareth, where He had been brought up, He went into the synagogue on the Sabbath day; and when the book of the prophet Isaiah was given to Him, He turned to the sixty-first chapter and began reading: "The Spirit of the Lord is upon me, because he hath anointed me to preach the gospel to the poor; he hath sent me to heal the broken-hearted, to preach deliverance to the captives, and recovering of sight to the blind, to set at liberty them that are bruised, to preach the acceptable year of the Lord." Then He closed the book, gave it again to the minister, and sat down. And the eyes of all who were in the synagogue were fastened on Him. And He began to say to them, "This day is this scripture fulfilled in your ears" (Luke 4:18–21). He saw Himself as the One of whom the prophet Isaiah spoke in this passage.

After His resurrection, He drew near to two sorrowing disciples who were walking from Jerusalem to Emmaus. The cause of their grief was their failure to see the sufferings of the Lord Jesus Christ in the Scriptures. They saw clearly that the Old Testament spoke of a Redeemer who would deliver Israel and set up an earthly kingdom, but they did not comprehend the passages which taught about the sufferings of the Messiah which must precede His kingdom.

The Lord Jesus Christ said to them, "O fools, and slow of heart to believe all that the prophets have spoken" (Luke 24:25). They believed just some of the verses which the prophets had spoken—those which revealed His glory—but they did not believe the verses which spoke of His cross. Our Lord rebuked them for not believing *all* that the prophets had spoken. "Ought not Christ to have suffered these things, and to enter into his glory?" The suffering must come first, and then the glory. "And beginning at Moses and all the prophets, he expounded unto them in all the scriptures the things concerning himself" (Luke 24:26,27).

How wonderful it must have been to hear Jesus expound His crucifixion from Psalm 22, Isaiah 53, and other passages—though they did not realize until later who this stranger was. How clearly Jesus saw both His sufferings and coming glory in the Word of God.

Later that day, He appeared to the terrified and frightened apostles hiding behind barred doors and comforted them with a similar exposition: "These are the words which I spake unto you, while I was yet with you, that all things must be fulfilled which were written in the law of Moses, and in the prophets, and in the psalms, concerning me" (Luke 24:44). Then He opened their minds to understand the Scriptures.

We will never see ourselves in the Word of God in the unique sense in which He did. He was the Son of God of whom the prophets wrote. However, should we not, in a very real way, see ourselves as we are revealed in the same Scriptures? Our salvation depends upon us seeing ourselves as we are revealed in the Word of God—poor, lost, vile, hopeless sinners, with no righteousness of our own, doomed to eternal hell. Then, too, the Scriptures reveal that all our sins were placed on Christ, and His death and resurrection were on our behalf. Salvation is offered to all, through repentance and faith in the Lord Jesus Christ. "For the wages of sin is death; but the gift of God is eternal life through Jesus Christ our Lord" (Romans 6:23). Each individual, if he is ever to be saved, must see himself in the Word of God as a poor, lost, hopeless sinner for whom Christ died and to whom Christ offers eternal salvation as a gift to be received by faith.

How much God has to show us in the Word concerning ourselves after we are born again! It seems that the entire Christian life is, in a sense, just a continuing revelation from the Word of God to us of our helplessness in ourselves and also of our abundant resources in Christ. Our spiritual growth is dependent upon seeing ourselves daily as we really are before God. We must see ourselves increasingly in the Word of God as weak vessels, defeated and nothing apart from Christ. Then, too, we must see ourselves in the Scriptures as crucified with Him, risen with Him, His life our life, His grace sufficient in our weakness.

We must learn that victory over sin is not by struggling against it in our own strength, but by reckoning ourselves "dead indeed unto sin, but alive unto God through Jesus Christ our Lord" (Romans 6:11). We count on this fact because we have learned from the Word of God that it is actually so. We were crucified with Him. The more we see in the Scriptures what we are by nature, and what we are

in union with Christ, then so much the more do we
learn to lay hold of Christ as our life and to have no
confidence in the flesh.

We learn too in the Scriptures of victory over the
world, the flesh, and the Devil. This victory has been
won for us by our Lord, and we enter into this
glorious victory by faith.

The great blessing of our daily meditations in the
Word is to see ourselves in our utter helplessness,
and also to see our complete sufficiency in Christ.
Each new day becomes a new experience of putting
off ourselves and putting on Christ.

IV. The Lord Jesus Christ Saw Current Events in
    the Light of the Scriptures.

The Lord Jesus Christ interpreted events in the
light of the Scriptures. This is the only proper way
to view any event. It is the only way we are able to
see any occurrence in its true light. Let us note His
practice of interpreting all events in the light of the
Scripture.

A. When the People Hardened Their Hearts to His
   Message.

When He met those who "seeing, see not, hearing,
they hear not, neither do they understand," instant-
ly Isaiah 6:9 and 10 came to His mind, and He said,
"In them is fulfilled the prophecy of Esaias, which
saith, By hearing ye shall hear, and shall not understand; and seeing ye shall see, and not perceive: for
this people's heart is waxed gross, and their ears are
dull of hearing, and their eyes they have closed; lest

at any time they should see with their eyes and hear with their ears, and should understand with their heart, and should be converted, and I should heal them" (Matthew 13:14, 15).

B. When the People Were Hypocritical.

The Jews used every device to get around the Word of God while at the same time pretending to love it and to keep it. When our Lord saw this, He said, "Ye hypocrites, well did Esaias prophesy of you, saying, This people draweth nigh unto me with their mouth, and honoreth me with their lips; but their heart is far from me" (Matthew 15:7,8). Our Lord was interpreting their actions in the light of Isaiah 29:13.

C. When He Was Hated by the Jews.

"He that hateth me hateth my Father also. If I had not done among them the works which none other man did, they had not had sin: but now have they both seen and hated both me and my Father. But this cometh to pass, that the word might be fulfilled that is written in their law, They hated me without a cause" (John 15:23–25).

When the enmity against Him was increasing, which finally led to His crucifixion, He saw it clearly in the light of Psalm 69:4. It was enmity without real reason for it. What a comfort to Him to have this baseless persecution interpreted for Him.

D. When the Children's Praises Aroused the Animosity of the Chief Priests and Scribes.

"And when the chief priests and scribes saw the wonderful things that he did, and the children crying in the temple, and saying, Hosanna to the son of David; they were sore displeased, and said unto him, Hearest thou what these say?" (Matthew 21:15,16). Immediately, this scene of the children crying "Hosanna to the son of David" recalled to His mind Psalm 8:2, and He answered, "Yea; have ye never read: Out of the mouth of babes and sucklings thou hast perfected praise?" (Matthew 21:16).

E. When He Was Rejected by the Jews.

The Lord Jesus told several parables, each of which revealed the same truth: that He would be rejected by the Jewish nation, and that as a result, God's crushing judgment would fall on them. In spite of their rejection of Him, God would honor and exalt Him. Jesus said unto them, "Did ye never read in the scriptures, The stone which the builders rejected, the same is become the head of the corner: this is the Lord's doing, and it is marvelous in our eyes?" (Matthew 21:42). He was quoting to them Psalm 118:22,23.

How necessary for Him to interpret in the light of the Scriptures His rejection by the Jewish builders, and thus to understand that even though He were the stone which the builders refused, God would yet exalt Him to become the headstone of the corner.

F. When He Was Forsaken by His Disciples.

Our Lord understood clearly the weakness in the hearts of the apostles which would lead them all eventually to forsake Him in the darkest hours of

His sufferings. He said unto them, "All ye shall be offended because of me this night: for it is written, I will smite the shepherd, and the sheep of the flock shall be scattered abroad" (Matthew 26:31). He was quoting Zechariah 13:7.

It must have strengthened our Lord in this time of great need to know about this forsaking in advance. It is not to be wondered, therefore, that it was written of Him, "He shall not fail nor be discouraged" (Isaiah 42:4). Our Lord saw all events of earth in control of His Father. He was moving down the pathway the Scriptures set for Him. He interpreted all events in the light of the Scriptures and so saw all events, as they truly are, under the control of God. This is the basic reason why He did not fail, nor was discouraged. What a comfort and sustaining power the Scriptures, which He knew so well, were to Him.

G. The Application of This Truth to Our Hearts.

Men's hearts fail them for fear today because they see the tragic events of earth apart from the Word of God, and of course, they see no solution to the world's crises. "And upon the earth distress of nations, with perplexity; the sea and the waves roaring; men's hearts failing them for fear, and for looking after those things which are coming on the earth" (Luke 21:25,26). The child of God instructed in the Word of God obeys the voice of the Lord who tells us, "And ye shall hear of wars and rumors of wars: see that you be not troubled: for all these things must come to pass" (Matthew 24:6). "And when these things begin to come to pass, then look up, and lift up your heads; for your redemption draweth nigh" (Luke 21:28).

The believer who feeds constantly upon the Word of God is not in the dark concerning current events. He has learned to interpret them in the light of the Scriptures. The result is the peace of God in his heart regardless of world conditions, and a quiet expectancy of the return of the Lord Jesus Christ. No wonder men's hearts fail them for fear when they have nothing to rely upon except poor, failing human wisdom and bankrupt, corrupt human resources. But as the Christian looks out upon world conditions, his heart will not fail him for fear if he is fortified by the Word of God and thus clearly sees that these conditions are already foretold. He sees history moving down the tracks of prophecy, and he knows that the coming of the Lord draws nigh.

It is certain that our Lord beholds the condition of earth today with its lawlessness, violence, and immorality. He sees the raging of the warring nations who, having rejected Him, are filled with fear as to the future, not knowing any way out. What our Lord sees does not disturb Him, because He has the solution to all the world's problems. If our Lord is not disturbed by the present world situation, then can it be His will that I, His child, be upset or disturbed by what I see around me?

The present world conditions are clearly foretold in the Scriptures.

1. The present wave of lawlessness is foretold in Matthew 24:12, which declares that iniquity (lawlessness) shall abound.
2. Immorality and crime are foretold in II Timothy 3:1–4.
3. The return of the Jew to Palestine is prophesied in Jeremiah 23:7,8, Luke 21:24, Isaiah

60:9, and Ezekiel 37:1–28.

4. The rise of Russia and her hostility to Israel, culminating in an attack against Israel, is foretold in Ezekiel 38 and 39.

5. The lukewarm condition of the wealthy, worldly professing church is foretold in Revelation 3:14–19.

6. The rise of the world church called "Mystery Babylon the Great, the mother of harlots" is presented in Revelation 17 and 18.

7. Destructive warfare with millions killed is prophesied in Revelation 6:8 and 9:15. Atomic weapons make this easily possible.

8. The activity of demons in leading many astray into false teaching and devil worship is prophesied in I Timothy 4:1.

These and many other alarming events which are occurring today with increasing intensity are clearly prophesied and interpreted for us in the Scriptures. The instructed Christian sees all these things clearly foretold in the Word of God and is not alarmed, distracted, hopeless, or worried. The Christian knows the coming of the Lord is drawing nigh. The Christian in heart-fellowship with Christ, living in vital union with Him, sees all these things in the Scriptures and—knowing the outcome of them—rests in the peace of God which passes all understanding.

V. The Lord Jesus Christ Used the Scriptures as a Weapon Against Satan.

Before our Lord began one act of public ministry, He was led by the Holy Spirit into the wilderness to be tempted of the devil. It was the devil's purpose to defeat Christ, and thus cancel any future ministry He might have. I would like to insert an observation at this point. I believe the power of Satan is especially concentrated on young people about to enter the service of the Lord. Intense temptations of a severe fleshly nature are hurled at them and many young people succumb. Scores of very promising young people in college and seminary have been sidetracked by yielding to severe temptation just as they were about to begin a life of ministry for the Lord.

The Lord Jesus Christ demonstrated the power inherent in the Word of God for overcoming the whole range of Satanic temptations. The Lord Jesus relied upon the same Word we have and upon which we should depend. He had this Word hidden in His heart, and the Holy Spirit could bring to His remembrance the very verses He needed in each crucial situation.

The first temptation was for Christ to satisfy the legitimate need of food in time of hunger. However, if our Lord had yielded to Satan's temptation, He would have been brought under the sway of the devil. It is always wrong to satisfy even a legitimate desire if the satisfaction of it brings us under Satanic control. The temptation was: "If thou be the Son of God, command that these stones be made bread" (Matthew 4:3). This temptation was met with Deuteronomy 8:3. "It is written, Man shall not live by bread alone, but by every word that proceedeth out of the mouth of God" (Matthew 4:4).

There is more to life than the mere satisfaction of eating food. It can never be the will of God even to take needed food in obedience to Satan. What terrible consequences would have followed if Christ had consented to such an act. It must not just be the need of bread to be considered, but is it bread in the will of God? Obedience to Satan in this temptation would be clearly out of the will of God. Therefore, the verse our Lord quoted was the sufficient and final answer.

The second temptation was an attack on Christ by Satan who quoted from the Word of God in which the Saviour trusted. However, Satan gave the wrong sense of the entire passage by leaving out an important part of the context. Satan said, "If thou be the Son of God, cast thyself down: for it is written, He shall give his angels charge concerning thee: and in their hands they shall bear thee up, lest at any time thou dash thy foot against a stone" (Matthew 4:6). Satan in quoting Psalm 91:11,12 left out the very important words "in all thy ways." God does not promise to protect His people in foolish, proud ventures out of His will.

He promises to keep His people as they walk in His way. It would be tempting God for our Lord to foolishly cast Himself down from the pinnacle of the temple and expect God to send angels to protect Him. The Lord Jesus met the temptation by citing Deuteronomy 6:16. "It is written again, Thou shalt not tempt the Lord thy God" (Matthew 4:7).

This is a very good lesson for Christians to learn. We are tempting God when we needlessly expose ourselves to dangers out of the will of God. We may even try to bolster our actions by a false interpretation of Scripture.

The third temptation was the attempt to get our Lord to receive the kingdoms of this world and the glory of them as a gift from Satan on the condition that our Lord fall down and worship him. Satan is

the ruler of the darkness of this world but he is also
a liar. However, even if Satan should keep his word
and relinquish whatever hold he had upon the
world, how could Christ be the sole ruler of the
world if He acknowledged Satan as an object of His
worship? The very thought of Christ being subject
to Satan is unthinkable and revolting. Satan promises so much to those who yield to him, but he never
gives his followers anything but bondage and corruption.

Our Lord quoted Deuteronomy 10:20, "Get thee
hence, Satan, for it is written, Thou shalt worship
the Lord thy God, and him only shalt thou serve"
(Matthew 4:10). There would be no bowing down
to Satan no matter how attractive the "offer." God
the Father was alone to be the object of His worship.

Our Lord won the victory over Satanic temptations by His use of the Word of God. There is much,
therefore, which we may learn from His experience.

We need to hide the Word of God in our hearts
for use when needed.

We are not to expect to be free from severe Satanic assaults.

There will always be a verse in the Word of God
to meet any Satanic attack.

The Lord Jesus Christ quoted the Scriptures in a
sense of a finality from which there could be no
appeal. This is exactly the way in which we should
rest upon the Scriptures when we have put the
Scriptures between us and a Satanic attack. Rest on
the authority of the Word.

The Word of God is more powerful than all the
varied temptations which Satan throws at us,
through appeals to the lust of the flesh, the lust of

the eyes, and the pride of life.

Once we have taken our stand upon the Word of God, Satan cannot get at us. He must recognize the superiority of the Word of God. He must leave, defeated by the Word. "I have written unto you, young men, because ye are strong, and the word of God abideth in you, and ye have overcome the wicked one" (I John 2:14).

VI. The Scriptures Were the Basis of His Actions.

Upon entering the temple, our Lord saw it defiled with the moneychangers and with those who sold doves. It had become, in His words, "a den of thieves" (Matthew 21:13). Immediately there flashed into His mind the words of Isaiah 56:7, "Mine house shall be called an house of prayer." This verse became the basis of His action as He cast the offenders out of the temple and overthrew their tables.

The Word of God should become the basis of our actions. There are actions in the light of present conditions which must be taken by the child of God, when the Scriptures are clear that such steps should be taken.

VII. The Lord Jesus Christ, When Praying, Made Use of Scripture in Addressing His Father.

When our Lord was rejected by the proud, sinful people of Chorazin, Bethsaida, and Capernaum, He thanked God in prayer because God had hidden these wonderful spiritual truths from the wise and prudent, and had revealed them unto babes (Matthew 11:25). Our Lord was using Psalm 8:2 in thanking God in that situation. Later, hanging upon the cross, forsaken by the Father, He made His cry of anguish to God in the words of Psalm 22:1, "My God, my God, why hast thou forsaken me?" His dying prayer, whereby He committed Himself to God, was Psalm 31:5, "Father, into thy hands I commend my spirit." What a wonderful way to go to be with the Father—with an appropriate verse of Scripture upon His lips.

The praying saints of God, likewise, filled their prayers with Scripture. Jehoshaphat, when in great peril due to the threatened invasion of the powerful Moabites and Ammonites, pleaded the record of Scripture as a basis for God to deliver him (II Chronicles 20:7-12).

Mary, in her song of praise to God for giving her the privilege of becoming the mother of Jesus, speaks her praise almost entirely in the words of Scripture (Luke 1:46-55).

Simeon, when he held the infant Jesus in his arms, breaks out in praise to God in the words of Scripture (Luke 2:25-35).

The early church was threatened by the Sanhedrin with persecution and death. The church went to God in this hour of crisis and prayed, using the words of the second Psalm (Acts 4:23-31).

The Christian today should be so filled with the Scriptures that the Holy Spirit can indicate to him what passages to use in pleading with God in prayer. How much lightness and near irreverence would thus be eliminated from our prayers. What great encouragement to believe God for the answer when we are praying on a scriptural basis.

May the Holy Spirit impress upon us the vital place the Scriptures had in the life of our Lord Jesus Christ. May He lead us to see that we can never be like Christ unless the Scriptures have a place of similar importance in our lives. May we realize our failure to perform this Christian duty and may the Holy Spirit work into our lives the power to enable us to follow the example of our Lord Jesus Christ in His attitude to the Scriptures.

How firm a foundation, ye saints of the Lord,
Is laid for your faith in His excellent Word.
What more can He say, than to you He hath said,
To you who for refuge to Jesus have fled?

Chapter 3

BEHOLD HIM IN DEPENDENCE UPON THE HOLY SPIRIT

The Lord Jesus Christ lived a life of complete dependence upon the Holy Spirit. In this, too, He becomes our great example. No child of God can possibly live a life pleasing to God apart from complete dependence upon the Holy Spirit.

I. He Was Anointed by the Holy Spirit for His Ministry.

"And Jesus, when he was baptized, went up straightway out of the water: and lo, the heavens were opened unto him, and he saw the Spirit of God descending like a dove, and lighting upon him: and lo a voice from heaven, saying, This is my beloved Son, in whom I am well pleased" (Matthew 3:16,17).

Before the Old Testament high priest began his ministry, he was anointed with the anointing oil. "Then shalt thou take the anointing oil, and pour it upon his head, and anoint him" (Exodus 29:7). This anointing with oil was an act of consecration of the Old Testament priests, setting them apart for their ministry.

The anointing of the Holy Spirit not only set

Jesus apart for the work of the ministry, but the presence of the Holy Spirit in His life was also the power of His ministry. "The word which God sent unto the children of Israel, preaching peace by Jesus Christ (he is Lord of all): that word, I say, ye know, which was published throughout all Judea, and began from Galilee, after the baptism which John preached; how God anointed Jesus of Nazareth with the Holy Ghost and with power: who went about doing good, and healing all that were oppressed of the devil; for God was with him" (Acts 10:36–38).

The Holy Spirit, likewise, sets apart Christians for definite duties in the will of God, and empowers them to carry out these responsibilities. As the believers in Antioch, "ministered to the Lord, and fasted, the Holy Ghost said, Separate me Barnabas and Saul for the work whereunto I have called them" (Acts 13:2). Barnabas and Saul ministered in the power of the Holy Spirit who had separated them unto Himself for definite missionary ministry. "Then Saul (who also is called Paul), filled with the Holy Ghost, set his eyes on him and said, O full of all subtilty and all mischief, thou child of the devil, thou enemy of all righteousness, wilt thou not cease to pervert the right ways of the Lord?" (Acts 13:9,10).

The ministry of the apostles was so under control of the Holy Spirit that even an apostle was not free to choose the place of his ministry. "Now when they [Paul with Silas and Timothy] had gone throughout Phrygia and the region of Galatia, and were forbidden of the Holy Ghost to preach the word in Asia, after they were come to Mysia, they assayed to go into Bithynia: but the Spirit suffered them not" (Acts 16:6,7).

The Holy Spirit definitely closed doors to the preaching of the gospel in places chosen by the apostles. Later, there came a clear call to carry the gospel to Europe. How important this decision that Europe was now to get the gospel. The history of Europe, America, and later the entire world was changed by the decision of the Holy Spirit to send the gospel at this time to Europe.

God has His complete plan for the evangelization of the world, and each believer has a particular place to minister in God's plan. To be in God's appointed place is to be where God is able to perform mighty miracles, bringing blessedness and fruitfulness into our lives. How important it is to permit the Holy Spirit to make all of the decisions relative to our ministry, in order that we may fit perfectly into God's plan.

II. The Holy Spirit Arranges a Severe Test for Christ.

We are told that Jesus was full of the Holy Ghost and that He was "led by the Spirit into the wilderness" (Luke 4:1). Mark used a very strong word denoting the leading of the Holy Spirit when he wrote, "And immediately the Spirit *driveth* him into the wilderness" (Mark 1:12).

The word "driveth" has in it the idea of forcing or impelling. The Holy Spirit was arranging a most severe test for Christ before He performed even one act of public ministry by driving Him into the wilderness to be tempted of the devil. These terrible assaults by Satan upon the Lord in the wilderness extended over a period of forty days.

The three temptations had one underlying purpose, to entice the Lord Jesus Christ to act independently of God.

It should be very clear to us that, even in seemingly legitimate things, Christ must never act independently of His Father. To satisfy any otherwise legitimate desire at Satan's suggestion apart from the will of God, would bring defeat into Christ's life, and bring Him into bondage to Satan. We can judge the severity of the assault by the necessity of angels afterward coming to strengthen Him physically (Mark 1:13).

The first temptation was an attempt to take advantage of the physical hunger of Christ. Satan said, "If thou be the Son of God, command that these stones be made bread" (Matthew 4:3). It is right to eat food when hungry, but never right to act under Satan's leadership to supply it. The need to satisfy bodily hunger was indeed present, but this need alone was not a sufficient basis for action. The will of God must be first considered. "Man shall not live by bread alone, but by every word that proceedeth out of the mouth of God," said Jesus, quoting Deuteronomy 8:3.

The second temptation was an appeal to perform a foolish and dangerous act, while at the same time claiming the protection of God. And so for us the desire to show the miracle power of God in our lives, protecting and caring for us, is a very legitimate aspiration. However, we must not tempt God by taking foolish risks out of His will.

Satan quoted Scripture as proof that Christ could cast Himself down from the pinnacle of the temple and no harm would come to Him. "For it is written, He shall give his angels charge concerning thee: and in their hands they shall bear thee up, lest at any time thou dash thy foot against a stone" (Matthew 4:6). However, in citing the passage, Satan omitted a controlling qualification, "to keep thee in all thy ways" (Psalm 91:11). Surely this promise did not apply to the present situation; since this was not the will of God, it could not be one of *His* ways. The Saviour answered, "It is written again, Thou shalt not tempt the Lord thy God." He was quoting Deuteronomy 6:16. It would be tempting God for Christ to do as Satan suggested.

The final attack dealt with the offer of the kingdoms of this world on the condition that the Lord Jesus Christ would fall down and worship Satan. The kingdoms of this world will some day be our Lord's (Revelation 11:15). He will get them because of His suffering on the cross (Psalm 2:6–8). Jesus repulsed Satan with the words, "It is written, Thou shalt worship the Lord thy God, and him only shalt thou serve" (Matthew 4:10). This truth is taught in Deuteronomy 10:20.

The victory over these temptations proved conclusively that the Saviour would never act independently of God and the Scriptures. He finished the severe test triumphantly, and was now ready to begin His public ministry.

Do not be surprised if, directly in the pathway of obedience to God, you find yourself in severe, crushing experiences. The Holy Spirit is interested in leading us into the circumstances which crush us and cause us to be cast upon God in more complete dependence. He will arrange and supervise such tests for us.

Jacob, the once fleshly schemer, had such a God-planned crushing experience—from which he emerged as Israel, a prince with God (Genesis 32:24–30). Luther said, "Two things make a real servant of God, prayer and temptation." No ministry is of value unless severely tried and tested. The more frequent and the more severe the trials in the will of God, the greater the usefulness that follows. It is well to look at these terrible testings as preludes to greater blessing and usefulness. We should learn to look upon these trials as coming from the Lord, with a gracious and fruitful design. Then we can look beyond the trial to God, and wait for Him to deliver us in His own time.

The biographies of men greatly used by God reveal that these men were permitted to suffer greatly for the Lord. Much of the blessing of their lives can be traced to the particular, supervised trials our Lord allowed. The greater and more frequent the trials we are willing to endure, the greater our usefulness in the hands of the Lord. The more severe and continued the suffering a Christian is called upon to endure, the greater usefulness and blessing he may expect from the Lord.

Years ago I read the following illustration of the greater usefulness which comes through suffering. "A bar of pig iron costs $1.00. If this bar is hammered into horseshoes, the value becomes $3.00. If the same bar of iron is refined and hammered into a steel sword, it is worth approximately $300.00. If this same bar of iron is further refined and drawn into watch springs, it becomes worth many thousands of dollars."

The purpose of all suffering and chastening is not, of course, for our destruction but "for our profit, that we might be partakers of his holiness." Although the chastening is not joyous, but grievous, "nevertheless afterward it yieldeth the peaceable fruit of righteousness unto them which are exercised thereby" (Hebrews 12:10,11). Suffering is necessary in order "that the trial of your faith, being much more precious than of gold that perisheth, though it be tried with fire, might be found unto praise and honor and glory at the appearing of Jesus Christ" (I Peter 1:7). It is well, therefore, in the midst of the trial, not only to say, "I am going to get out of this difficulty," but also to say, "I am going to get great *profit* out of it."

III. The Lord Jesus Christ Continued in the Power of the Holy Spirit.

We read that, after His glorious victory over Satan, "Jesus returned in the power of the Spirit into Galilee: and there went out a fame of him through all the region round about" (Luke 4:14).

It is so easy for Christians, after experiencing a great victory through the power of God, to ease off into self-confidence, and to continue not in the power of the Spirit but in the power of the flesh. We see this so well illustrated in the Apostle Peter. How quickly after uttering that great confession, "Thou art the Christ, the Son of the living God," were Peter's lips used by Satan to say, "Be it far from thee, Lord: this shall not be unto thee" (Matthew 16:16,22). Peter was rebuking the Lord Jesus Christ because our Lord spoke of the necessity of His coming death and resurrection. Peter surely did not continue in the power of the Spirit. On one occasion, his lips were used to utter a great revelation from God; but shortly thereafter, the same lips were used to utter words suggested by Satan.

Elijah is another illustration of the fact that even men greatly blessed by God may fail to continue walking with Him. Elijah won a great victory on Mount Carmel where alone he defeated the four hundred and fifty false prophets of Baal and the four hundred false prophets of the groves. His victory was because of complete reliance upon the Lord. Listen to his prayer: "Lord God of Abraham, Isaac, and of Israel, let it be known this day that thou art God in Israel, and that I am thy servant, and that I have done all these things at thy word. Hear me, O Lord, hear me, that this people may know that thou art the Lord God, and that thou hast turned their heart back again" (I Kings 18:36,37). Then the fire of the Lord fell. But it was not too long after this that we find Elijah under the juniper tree, having fled there in fear of Jezebel's threats upon his life. He pleads with God that he might die, complaining that "It is enough." Elijah is in the depths of despair and self-pity, occupied with himself and not with God. He overemphasizes his own work and fails to see God working anywhere else. Obviously he has not continued in the power of the Spirit. His words under the juniper tree are not the words of a man relying upon the power of God. Yet who among us, even after a great victory, has not been subject to similar thoughts of discouragement and unbelief.

King Uzziah of Judah is yet another sad example of one who, once walking in the power of God, did not continue in this power but went off, instead, in the power of the flesh. Under God's direction this great king did many notable things in the early years of his reign. "And he sought God in the days of

Zechariah, who had understanding in the visions of God: and as long as he sought the Lord, God made him to prosper" (II Chronicles 26:5). "And his name spread far abroad; for he was marvelously helped, till he was strong. But when he was strong, his heart was lifted up to his destruction: for he transgressed against the Lord his God, and went into the temple of the Lord to burn incense upon the altar of incense" (II Chronicles 26:15,16). After experiencing the wonderful power of God because of his yieldedness to the Lord, Uzziah, now being lifted up with pride, acted in defiance of God. Azariah, the chief priest, and eighty other priests pleaded with him not to continue in his act of rebellion. However, in his pride he was determined to exercise the functions which God would have His priests alone perform. He persisted in his self-will and was stricken by God with leprosy, and had to live in a separate place until the day of his death. He died a leper. Surely Uzziah did not continue to walk in the power of God.

This little sentence "And Jesus returned in the power of the Spirit" contains a most blessed teaching for each child of God. Each pastor would do well to repeat this verse to himself as he returns to the parsonage after the day's ministry. If the pastor believes he has seen real blessing, how usual it is to be elated, and to return in the power of self-confidence. Then it becomes very easy to feel one can just coast into further victories. Prayer and Bible reading are apt to be less urgent. This is fatal to the spiritual life. On the other hand, the pastor may feel his efforts have been poor, the attendance low, with little or no liberty in preaching. It is easy at such times to return in the power of despair, discouragement, and defeat. It will be a cause for real blessing, therefore, if the pastor will say quietly and simply after each Lord's day ministry, "I will return in the power of the Spirit."

This principle of continuing in the power of the Holy Spirit is one which must be observed throughout our entire Christian lives. Paul writes to the Galatians and asks them, "Are ye so foolish? having begun in the Spirit, are ye now made perfect by the flesh? have ye suffered so many things in vain? if it be yet in vain" (Galatians 3:3,4).

To the very last day we live, to the very last breath we breathe, we are to continue in the power of the Holy Spirit and never to live in the power of the self-life. It is impossible for the self-life to complete anything begun by the Spirit of God. May God give us grace to continue in the power of the Spirit, until we see Him.

IV. The Holy Spirit and the Public Ministry of the Lord Jesus Christ.

The public ministry of the Lord Jesus Christ was entirely in the power of the Holy Spirit. He did not minister independently of the Spirit of God.

When He entered the synagogue in His home village of Nazareth, the book of the prophet Isaiah was delivered to Him. He opened it at the sixty-first chapter and began to read, "The Spirit of the Lord is upon me, because he hath anointed me to preach the gospel to the poor; he hath sent me to heal the broken-hearted, to preach deliverance to the captives, and recovering of sight to the blind, to set at liberty them that are bruised, to preach the acceptable year of the Lord." And He closed the scroll, gave it again to the attendant, and sat down. And the eyes of all those who were in the synagogue were fastened on Him. And He began to say unto them, "This day is this scripture fulfilled in your ears" (Luke 4:16–21).

Jesus declared that the powerful ministry which He was to perform would be made possible because of the Spirit of the Lord upon Him. The secret of His ministry was the power of the Holy Spirit.

Peter, in his sermon to the Gentiles in the home of Cornelius, tells us the same truth: the secret of the ministry of the Lord Jesus was the presence and power of the Holy Spirit in His life. "God anointed Jesus of Nazareth with the Holy Ghost and with power: who went about doing good, and healing all that were oppressed of the devil; for God was with him" (Acts 10:38).

The Lord Jesus spoke of the power by which He cast out demons as being the power of the Spirit of God. "But if I cast out demons by the Spirit of God, then the kingdom of God is come unto you" (Matthew 12:28).

John declared that the Lord Jesus Christ spoke the words of God because "God giveth not the Spirit by measure unto him. The Father loveth the Son, and hath given all things into his hand" (John 3:34,35). The very words the Lord Jesus uttered were words in the power of the Holy Spirit. Therefore, He could say, "It is the spirit that quickeneth; the flesh profiteth nothing: the words that I speak unto you, they are spirit, and they are life" (John 6:63).

How extremely important it is that each believer should minister the Word of God in the power of the Holy Spirit. The Apostle Paul, in describing his ministry among the Corinthians, said he did not come to them in excellency of speech or wisdom, nor did he use persuasive words of man's wisdom. Extremely conscious of his own weakness and in fear and trembling, but in dependence upon the Holy Spirit, he preached the gospel. His entire dependence upon the Holy Spirit had blessed results. "My preaching," Paul said, was "in demonstration of the Spirit and of power, that your faith should not stand in the wisdom of men, but in the power of God" (I Corinthians 2:1–5).

All ministry of the Word other than that which is in the power of the Holy Spirit is futile. The flesh can accomplish nothing. Not even brilliant, clever, educated, oratorical flesh can move anyone toward God. As a result of Paul's preaching, the Holy Spirit so convinced the hearers of the truth of the message that they were certain God had spoken to them, and their faith stood therefore in the power of God.

Each servant of God should desire so to speak that, because of his message, the people will be drawn supernaturally to God by the Holy Spirit. Andrew Murray points out from the words of Jesus that this convicting power of the Holy Spirit is to flow through believers. "It is expedient for you that I go away: for if I go not away, the Comforter will not come unto you; but if I depart, I will send him unto you. And when he is come [unto you], he will reprove the world of sin, and of righteousness, and of judgment" (John 16:7,8).

The Apostle Paul also called to the attention of the Thessalonian believers that his ministry there was not in mere words but in the power of the Holy Spirit. "For our gospel came not unto you in word only, but also in power, and in the Holy Ghost, and in much assurance" (I Thessalonians 1:5).

The tremendous results of this Spirit-filled preaching are enumerated in verses six to ten of First Thessalonians one: the Thessalonians became followers of the Lord, endured affliction, had the joy of the Holy Ghost, became examples for other believers, sent out the Word of God to others, and having turned from idols to serve the living and the true God, were waiting for His Son to return from heaven. If *we* are ever to have results such as these, our ministry of the Word of God *also* must be in the power of the Holy Ghost. Paul said, "Our gospel came not to you in word only." How often we have been led to feel the gospel we preached came in word only, without the power of the Holy Spirit. How different when the power of the Holy Spirit accompanies the preaching of the gospel!

Just to know the facts of the gospel does not give one the needed power to preach these facts. The apostles and other believers were eyewitnesses of the crucifixion and resurrection of the Lord Jesus Christ. They had all the facts, yet they were commanded to wait before they began preaching—to wait until they would be endued with power from on high. "But ye shall receive power after that the Holy Ghost is come upon you: and ye shall be witnesses unto me" (Acts 1:8). When the Holy Ghost came on the day of Pentecost, then they preached the gospel facts in the power of the Holy Ghost, with supernatural results.

A preaching of even the truth without the power of the Holy Spirit tends to harden people to the gospel, and certainly brings no blessing upon the hearers. It should be the passion of those who minister the Word of God to seek earnestly the power of the Holy Ghost upon each message. There should be a willingness to pay any price, or to remove any hindrance to His working through us.

Dr. Horace Dean gave an illustration years ago that I have never forgotten. He told of being in Canada with some other men. After a tiresome hike, they had become very thirsty. A sign was noticed on a tree, directing to a spring. They went to where the spring was supposed to be—but found just damp leaves. However, by digging out the leaves and removing much debris that had been clogging the spring, they discovered the water and it was soon flowing again in refreshing power.

The Holy Spirit desires greatly to flow through us in power to others in need. "He that believeth on me, as the scripture hath said, out of his innermost being shall flow rivers of living water. But this spake he of the Spirit" (John 7:38,39, margin). Sin, worldliness, or unyieldedness on any point, no matter how trivial we may think it is, clogs up the Spring within. We cease to be a blessing to others because the water of the Holy Spirit within us is not permitted to flow through us.

The Holy Spirit did not come into our temple, as it were, empty-handed. He came with gifts for each believer. These are to enable us to minister, and thus to fill a particular need in the body of Christ. All true ministry is, therefore, allowing the Holy Spirit to so possess us that we are enabled to minister the gifts with which He has so richly endowed us. "Now there are diversities of gifts, but the same Spirit" (I Corinthians 12:4). "As every man hath received the gift, even so minister the same one to another, as good stewards of the manifold grace of God" (I Peter 4:10).

V. The Holy Spirit and the Cross.

"Christ, who through the eternal Spirit offered himself without spot to God" (Hebrews 9:14). In this statement concerning the cross, we see the Father, Son, and Holy Spirit mentioned. Christ, the Son of God, was enabled in the power of the Holy Spirit to offer Himself without spot to God the Father. The Holy Spirit led Him in complete obedience unto death, even the death of the cross. He offered Himself as a sacrifice to God in the power of the Holy Spirit.

The Holy Spirit will lead each Christian to the cross for the crucifixion of the flesh with its affections and lusts. He will teach the earnest believer who desires freedom from the power of the flesh and of sin the truth that the believer has been crucified with Christ in order that, henceforth, he should not serve sin. Victory over sin is not a matter of struggling to overcome it, nor is it by eradication of the old sinful nature, but by reckoning on the fact that in Christ we are "dead indeed unto sin, but alive unto God" (Romans 6:11). Victory will be experienced when struggle ceases, and we quietly reckon upon the fact that we are dead to sin and alive unto God through Jesus Christ our Lord. The Holy Spirit will lead us to the cross to show us how to be delivered from our self-life, and He will enlighten us as to what happened there in order that we might be delivered. He will enable us in our daily experience to die to sin and to live unto God.

When still a young Christian, I was greatly troubled and defeated by an inability to put out of my life something which God said should go. It was not unwillingness, but ignorance as to how to be delivered. Severe struggle meant hours of defeat and agony as self was helpless to cast out the self life. It was my custom in the early evening to take a walk with my Bible as my companion. The Spirit of God, I am sure, led me to read Romans 6. If I read it once, I must have read this chapter at least fifty times during this struggle. One evening, sitting on a log on the bank of the Wissahickon Creek, my eyes rested upon Romans 6:11, "likewise reckon ye also yourselves to be dead indeed unto sin, but alive unto God through Jesus Christ our Lord." I cannot explain what happened except that the Holy Spirit made that verse real to me. All struggle ceased and I walked up out of that valley free. Many years have passed since that memorable experience, but the way of victory over sin has not changed. It is by reckoning ourselves to be dead indeed unto sin but alive unto God through Jesus Christ our Lord. I have come to see, as the years have passed, more of the depth of the meaning of our crucifixion with Christ. We are dead to every form of every sin, and we are called upon to make this fact real in our experience by simply reckoning it to be so. Dead men do not sin. "For he that is dead is freed from sin" (Romans 6:7). If a man had been a hopeless slave to the sin of drunkenness, and he is now dead, it would be possible to put the most enticing liquor close to him and he would now make no response, because he is dead. This is the position of the Christian regarding all sin. We are dead with Christ to all sin.

Why then do Christians sin? we may ask. The answer is simple. It is because when temptations come, we are alive to the sin instead of reckoning ourselves dead to it. This reckoning of ourselves to be dead to sin may require a conscious effort at first, but later it will become almost automatic to immediately reckon ourselves dead to the temptation which confronts us, and to reckon ourselves alive unto God.

In the measure that the Holy Spirit is permitted to put the self-life to death in all its various manifestations, in that measure will we experience the resurrection power and life of Christ. We must allow the Holy Spirit to lead to the place of death the secret, sinful transactions of our hearts. Images and scenes of the heart which grieve the Holy Spirit must be taken to the place of death. The Holy Spirit will lead us to the cross in order that we may appropriate what the Lord did for us there. "For if ye live after the flesh, ye shall die: but if ye through the Spirit do mortify the deeds of the body, ye shall live" (Romans 8:13). "This I say then, Walk in the Spirit, and ye shall not fulfil the lust of the flesh" (Galatians 5:16). We have been commanded to be filled with the Holy Spirit (Ephesians 5:18).

VI. Results of the Spirit-Filled Life.

In closing this chapter on the Holy Spirit, it may be well to give a few blessed results of the Spirit-filled life. It has been well said, "There is no problem to the Christian beyond yieldedness to the Holy Spirit." The Holy Spirit, who indwells every believer, will, when yielded to, fill the believer and become Lord of his life. The Holy Spirit will:

Be the power of the prayer life (Romans 8:26).

Give constant victory over sin (Galatians 5:16, Romans 8:13).

Reveal the Lord Jesus Christ (John 16:14,15).

Guide (Romans 8:14).

Sanctify (II Corinthians 3:18).

Enable the believer to witness boldly for Christ (Acts 1:8, 4:31).

Create Christian character (Galatians 5:22,23).

Use the gifts with which He has endowed each believer (I Corinthians 12).

Flow through yielded Christians (John 7:38,39).

How necessary, therefore, for each Christian to live a life of complete dependence upon the Holy Spirit, beholding the example of the Lord Jesus Christ.

Thou canst fill me, gracious Spirit,
    Though I cannot tell Thee how;
But I need Thee, greatly need Thee,
    Come, oh, come and fill me now.

I am weakness, full of weakness;
    At Thy sacred feet I bow;
Blest divine, eternal Spirit
    Fill with power, and fill me now.

—E. H. Stokes

Chapter 4

BEHOLD HIM IN DOING THE FATHER'S WILL

The Lord Jesus Christ gave Himself up utterly to do the will of God. What a joy to meditate upon this life, so given to God for the Father's will. We must see in His complete yieldedness to the will of God the perfect example for us.

I. He Declared He Came Into the World to Do the Will of God.

"Then said I, Lo, I come . . . to do thy will, O God" (Hebrews 10:7).

The blood of bulls and goats can never take away sins, therefore in burnt offerings and sacrifices for sin, God had no pleasure (Hebrews 10:4,6). Christ, therefore, did not come into the world to offer further animal sacrifices. He had a body prepared by God in which He came to do the will of God. It was God's will for Christ to offer His own body as the one sacrifice which would forever put away sin. He "put away sin by the sacrifice of himself" (Hebrews 9:26). A prepared body, a yielded will—this characterized Him as He entered this world.

God's will meant not only the offering of His body as a sacrifice for sin to make salvation possible, but also the preservation of all those saved by this offering. "For I came down from heaven, not to do mine own will, but the will of him that sent me. And this is the Father's will which hath sent me, that of all which he hath given me I should lose nothing, but should raise it up again at the last day" (John 6:38,39).

Let us keep before us this great truth that as the Lord Jesus Christ entered the world He said, "Lo, I come . . . to do thy will, O God" (Hebrews 10:7).

II. The Father's Will Was His Constant Delight.

"I delight to do thy will, O my God: yea, thy law is within my heart" (Psalm 40:8).

Each new revelation of the Father's will brought added delight to Him. There was such an eagerness to do the Father's will that there was no interval between knowing the Father's will and actually doing it. It is to the shame of us Christians that so often we live in that awful interval which lies between knowing God's will and actually doing it. When the unyielded Christian insists on holding back from doing God's known will, this Christian is on the way to defeat and barrenness. Even the yielded Christian, however, does not always delight in the Father's will, especially at the first revelation of a new leading. The parable of the two sons as recorded in Matthew 21:28–30 illustrates this. Though the first son eventually did his father's will, he was unwilling to do it at the outset.

The Lord Jesus Christ, however, as soon as He knew the will of God, no matter how costly, delighted in it and did it. The Father's will was His whole joy; He had no joy apart from it. Never for a moment did He swerve from it.

III. The Father's Will Was His Meat.

"My meat is to do the will of him that sent me, and to finish his work" (John 4:34).

The Lord Jesus Christ, though weary and hungry, sat by the wellside at Sychar in order to win a wayward woman to Himself. The disciples had previously gone away into the city to buy provisions. When they returned, they marveled that He would talk with such a woman; yet, no one apparently had the courage to question Him concerning it. The woman hurried into the city to carry the joyful news of having found the Messiah. In the meantime, His disciples urged Him to eat. But He replied, "I have meat to eat that ye know not of" (John 4:32). Winning this woman to Himself, and thus to salvation, was in the will of the Father and part of the work the Father sent Him to do.

The Lord Jesus Christ had a supply of spiritual nourishment and support at this moment unknown to the disciples. The joy and blessing of doing the Father's will had for a time lifted Him above the consciousness of any bodily needs. He was so refreshed that He was strengthened physically.

A Christian in the will of God has a supply of spiritual nourishment that can also be felt in a revived body. This secret supply of strength is unknown to the worldling or to people who know the Lord but do not do His complete will. How frequently a believer has testified that a weak body had actually been strengthened by taking a definite step in the will of God. "I felt too weak to come to prayer meeting tonight, but I came anyway because I believed it to be God's will. How different I feel now; even my body feels the blessing of this meeting. I have been lifted up both spiritually and physically." This has been the frequent testimony of people who did the will of God.

So it should be with each believer as with Christ: that which satisfies, sustains, and nourishes us is the blessing of doing the will of God.

IV. He Sought the Father's Will.

"I can of mine own self do nothing: as I hear, I judge: and my judgment is just; because I seek not mine own will, but the will of the Father which hath sent me" (John 5:30).

He actively sought the Father's will as one seeks a great treasure. He would do nothing independently of His Father's will, whether speaking or judging. No thoughts, no desires, no motives were to originate in Himself or to be for Himself. All He did was in harmony with the Father's will.

The Father's will was not something learned once and for all, but the present tense of the verb indicates a constant, continual seeking. This accounts for the early morning and all night vigils of prayer and meditation in the presence of the Father.

The Lord Jesus Christ never exercised His will independently of the Father. He had no private interest. "Verily, verily, I say unto you, The Son can do nothing of himself, but what he seeth the Father do: for what things soever he doeth, these also doeth the Son likewise" (John 5:19).

It was the pleasure of the Lord which prospered

in his hands (Isaiah 53:10).

The Christian should actively seek the Father's will. The late Dr. A. W. Tozer wrote a book entitled *The Pursuit of God*. In a real sense, Christians should daily pursue God in order to lay hold upon God. We must take time to let God search the heart and should wait for each leading further into His will. This seeking and walking in the will of God is to continue throughout the believer's entire life, even to the last conscious breath. There should be an active pursuit of God on behalf of the Christian, even in old age. "They shall still bring forth fruit in old age" (Ps. 92:14). "And even to your old age I am he; and even to hoar hairs will I carry you: I have made, and I will bear; even I will carry, and will deliver you" (Isaiah 46:4).

These verses indicate the blessing shown to all those who seek the will of God constantly. They will still be fruitful even in old age and will enjoy the protection and care of the Lord.

To be like Christ requires an active, daily seeking of the will of God.

V. Gethsemane: The Supreme Test.

We approach the scene in the Garden of Gethsemane with reverence and awe. The Holy Spirit has seen fit to indicate to us, for our profit, somewhat of the awful struggle that was taking place there. The descriptions the Gospel writers give us of Christ in Gethsemane are very instructive. Matthew tells us He was sorrowful and very heavy—sorrowful even unto death. Mark says He was greatly amazed, sore troubled, and fell on His face. Luke declares He was in an agony, and prayed earnestly, and His sweat was as it were great drops of blood falling down to the ground.

What was the reason for our Lord being in such intense spiritual suffering—so great that it weakened Him physically? It is not possible to penetrate the deep and sacred mystery of all that caused the suffering in Gethsemane. However, the Scriptures are clear that upon the Holy One of God was about to be placed the sin of the world. "The Lord hath laid on him the iniquity of us all" (Isaiah 53:6). The comment of F. C. Jennings upon this passage will enable us to see more clearly the horror to Christ of bearing the sin of the world: "Here we look at what the highest of created intelligences consider with profound amazement, and they ever desire to fathom those unfathomable depths still further: That God, the very God from whom every one of us has wandered afar although in different directions, should Himself cause the iniquities of us all to meet as myriads of foul, black sewers might meet, and in one awful rushing, filthy, malodorous flood empty itself at one spot on His Son, the dearest object of His own heart."

Our hatred of sin is in proportion to the holiness of our lives. Before we were saved, it did not cause some of us too much inner pain to take that Holy Name in vain. However, after being saved and being enabled to love the Lord Jesus, what pain it caused us even to hear that worthy Name blasphemed by someone else.

No man hated sin as did the Lord Jesus Christ because no one was as holy as He. "Thou hast loved righteousness, and hated iniquity" (Hebrews 1:9). Our hearts shudder to think, even with our very limited understanding, what horror it must have caused the holy Son of God to realize that He was about to be made sin. Never was one so holy as this One, and He was about to have placed upon Him the sin of the whole world.

In the midst of His extreme agony, His one desire is the Father's will. "O my Father, if this cup may not pass away from me, except I drink it, thy will be done" (Matthew 26:42). "If thou be willing, remove this cup from me: nevertheless not my will, but thine, be done" (Luke 22:42). This prayer, uttered three times, reveals Christ even in His intense suffering never moving from, nor desiring anything else but, the Father's will.

"Who in the days of his flesh, when he had offered up prayers and supplications with strong crying and tears unto him that was able to save him from [out of] death, and was heard in that he feared; though he were a Son, yet learned he obedience by the things which he suffered" (Hebrews 5:7,8). This verse does not teach us that He was ever *dis*obedient, but that in suffering He learned all that was *involved* in obedience. He "became obedient unto death, even the death of the cross" (Philippians 2:8). He had learned in Gethsemane that He must drink the cup. He sees the cup now coming from the Father's hand, and declares, when Peter and others would deliver Him from the Roman soldiers who came to arrest Him, "The cup which my Father hath given me, shall I not drink it?" (John 18:11).

J. C. Ryle remarks: "Warm feelings and joy are not the truest evidence of the grace of God. A will given over to God is far more valuable evidence. Our Lord did not always rejoice, but He did always say 'Thy will be done.'"

The sacrifice of our wills is what God desires most from us, even submission to pain and death if He so will. The will of God was dearer to Christ than His own will, even though God's will meant His death on the cross and involved such intense spiritual and physical suffering.

The Christian must learn from beholding Christ how to face the supreme tests in life. No matter how costly God's will seems to be, even if it should cost our lives, our one response should be, "Not my will, but Thy will be done."

VI. The Time Schedule of the Lord Jesus Christ Was in the Will of God.

One of the most marvelous blessings of being in the will of God is to move on the Father's time schedule. The Lord Jesus Christ learned that He must not only do the Father's will, but that He must perform each act in the Father's will at the exact time the Father decreed.

When the Lord Jesus Christ came forth from eternity into a world of time, these words could express His thoughts, "My times are in thy hand" (Psalm 31:15). The ordering of His moments, hours, and days was in God's hand. His coming into the world, the events of the life He lived here, and even His death were all on the Father's time schedule.

"But when the fulness of the time was come, God sent forth his Son, made of a woman, made under the law" (Galatians 4:4). When the proper time had come for our redemption, God sent forth His Son.

The lesson was given quite early in His life that He was to be on the Father's time schedule: "Be thou there *until* I bring thee word" (Matthew 2:13). These words were uttered by the angel of the Lord to Mary and Joseph who were ordered to flee with the young Christ Child to Egypt to escape the murderous designs of Herod. They were to stay in Egypt living in a strange country under difficult circumstances, until the time God told them it was safe to return.

During His adult life He also moved on the Father's timing. He did not move even on the schedule suggested by His loved ones. Our loved ones do not necessarily have the will of God for us, as sincere and thoughtful as they may be. For instance, at the wedding feast in Cana of Galilee, Jesus' mother said to Him, "They have no wine" (John 2:3). As if to say, "Surely, the time is come to declare Thyself, to manifest Thy miracle power and glory. I know Thee, but they do not." The Lord Jesus Christ answered her, "Woman, what have I to do with thee? Mine hour is not yet come" (John 2:4).

Addressing His mother with the word "woman" is not to be considered harsh, but is the very word later used in great tenderness and consideration when, as He hung upon the cross, He committed His mother into John's care. These words, however, surely indicate a tremendous difference between the Lord Jesus Christ and His mother. "What have we in common when you consider our persons? I am creator God; you are but a creature. My time to do this miracle is not yet. I am on my Father's time now."

In the previous years as a child He had been subject to Mary. But now, as He begins His lifework in the will of God, He is not dependent on the suggestions of Mary, His mother. The so-called "intercession of Mary" is error. Henceforth she must allow our Lord to choose the Father's time to act.

Later He announced to His unbelieving brethren that He was on the Father's time schedule. Surely, worldly people with worldly motives could not possibly have the mind of God for Jesus. His unbelieving brethren urged Him to go to Jerusalem to the Feast of Tabernacles, there to display Himself and make an impression upon the people. These were the hypocritical and insincere words of brethren who did not believe in Him (John 7:3-5). The Lord Jesus Christ answered, "Go ye up unto the feast: I go not up yet unto this feast; for my time is not yet full come" (John 7:8).

Later, after His brethren were gone up, He went up to the feast. He was very careful to be on the Father's time, even when only a little time was involved.

A few moments or hours can make an eternal difference if we are not in the place where God would have us be.

No one could upset the Father's time program for the Lord Jesus Christ. Luther said, "The devil shoots at the clock, but in vain." The enemies of the Lord had the will to hurt, but not the power. "Then they sought to take him: but no man laid hands on him, because his hour was not yet come" (John 7:30). There was a divine restraint which rendered them helpless. The hour had not yet come for Him to leave this world, and there was a fixed time during which our Lord's ministry was to last. His ministry at this point was not yet finished.

In John 8:20 we read a similar statement of the helplessness of murderous men due to the Father's timing concerning His Son: "These words spake Jesus in the treasury, as he taught in the temple: and no man laid hands on him, for his hour had not yet come."

His death occurred on the Father's time. When the appointed time drew near for Him to be crucified, resurrected, and then received up into heaven, we read, "And it came to pass, when the time was come that he should be received up, he stedfastly set his face to go to Jerusalem" (Luke 9:51). He was moving toward Jerusalem to be there on the Father's time.

Arriving in Jerusalem, He faced His last week on earth. He said, "Now is my soul troubled; and what shall I say? Father, save me from this hour: but for this cause came I unto this hour. Father, glorify thy name." Then came there a voice from heaven, saying, "I have both glorified it, and will glorify it again" (John 12:27,28). As He thought upon the coming Passion, He experienced a sudden strong mental agony. It was not the prospect of physical death which troubled Him but the burden of man's sin, the prospect of bearing the weight of the world's guilt. Yet He could not pray for deliverance from the hour because He had reached this very hour for the intention of suffering death, even the death of the cross.

Later in the week, He began His great high priestly prayer with the words, "Father, the hour is come" (John 17:1). Oh, the meaning in these words! The hour had come in God's eternal counsels for the sacrifice of His Son, and the Sacrifice was now ready. The hour had arrived for the fulfillment of the great promise that the seed of the woman would bruise the head of the serpent (Genesis 3:15). This was one of the greatest hours of all history.

He went out from Gethsemane in the hands of

sinners. They were now permitted to take Him because His hour had come. The Lord Jesus Christ said to His sleeping apostles, "Sleep on now, and take your rest: it is enough, the hour is come; behold, the Son of Man is betrayed into the hands of sinners" (Mark 14:41). Our Lord did not fall into the enemies' hands through inability to escape, but because the hour had come for Him to be in the sinners' hands to be crucified. "Him, being delivered by the determinate counsel and foreknowledge of God, ye have taken, and by wicked hands have crucified and slain" (Acts 2:23). He died on the Father's time, the appropriate and appointed time. "In due time Christ died for the ungodly" (Romans 5:6).

What is the application of all this to the believer's heart? It is, briefly, that as the Father had a will for Christ and He lived utterly for it, moving on the Father's time, even so, this is God's will for every believer.

We see God's perfect timing in causing Philip, who was sent down from Samaria and was on the way to Gaza, to meet the Ethiopian returning from Jerusalem. This meeting resulted in the Ethiopian's salvation (Acts 8:26–29), and Africa received the gospel. How important is this timing by God. At just the proper time, God caused the servant of Abraham, who was seeking a bride for Isaac, to meet Rebekah at the well (Genesis 24:12–15). What an important link in God's program for Israel.

VII. Self-will Is Rebellion Against God's Will and Is Therefore Sin.

Self-will in Lucifer marked the beginning of sin in

the universe. Self-will in Lucifer grew out of self-occupancy. "Thine heart was lifted up because of thy beauty" (Ezekiel 28:17). Lucifer's heart was lifted up when he became occupied with what God had made him instead of being occupied with God. Self-occupancy leads to that self-expression which is rebellion against God's will. "How art thou fallen from heaven, O Lucifer, son of the morning! how art thou cut down to the ground, which didst weaken the nations! For thou hast said in thine heart, *I will* ascend into heaven, *I will* exalt my throne above the stars of God: *I will* sit also upon the mount of the congregation, in the sides of the north: *I will* ascend above the heights of the clouds; *I will* be like the Most High. Yet thou shalt be brought down to hell, to the sides of the pit" (Isaiah 14:12–15).

It is dangerous for a believer to become occupied with the gifts which God has given him. This, also, can lead easily to that self-occupancy from which self-expression, independent of God, proceeds. When Lucifer became so absorbed with his own beauty, his heart was lifted up and five times he uttered his "I will" of defiance to God. God could not, even for an instant, tolerate this rebellion, and Lucifer was judged and cast out of heaven.

There is nothing worse than self-will. No one in the universe has a right to express a will contrary to God's will. Our highest joy is in saying constantly from the heart, "Not my will but Thine be done." Self-will is the mark of each unregenerate child of Adam. "All we like sheep have gone astray; we have turned every one to *his own* way" (Isaiah 53:6).

The degree to which it is possible for self-will to control any unsaved person may be seen by referring to a certain Louis Blanc. He died upon the scaffold for his crime. He had boasted: "When I was an infant I rebelled against my nurse. When I was a child I rebelled against my teachers. When I was a young man I rebelled against my father. When I was of mature years I rebelled against the law. When I die, and if there is a heaven and a God, I will rebel against Him."

Self-will is also prominent in the believer who walks in the power of the flesh instead of the power of the Holy Spirit. There is nothing which brings so much misery into the life as self-will. J. C. Ryle said, "A will unsanctified and uncontrolled is the one great cause of unhappiness in life." The many Christians who have become fruitless castaways bear abundant testimony to the unalterable fact that it does not pay to have one's way in defiance to God.

VIII. God Saves Us in Order That We Might Know and Do His Will.

"The God of our fathers hath chosen thee, that thou shouldest know his will" (Acts 22:14).

There is the will of God for each believer, and it is each believer's duty to understand it and to do it. "Wherefore be ye not unwise, but understanding what the will of the Lord is" (Ephesians 5:17). "That he no longer should live the rest of his time in the flesh to the lusts of men, but to the will of God" (I Peter 4:2). Each believer is to serve his own generation with its definite needs by the will of God. It is said of David, "After he had served his own generation by the will of God, [he] fell on sleep, and was laid unto his fathers" (Acts 13:36).

It may be asked, How am I to know the will of God for my life? There is much revealed to us in the Word of God of the clear will of God for each believer. Such verses as I Thessalonians 4:3–7, 5:18, I Peter 2:11–15, 3:17, 4:19, and Galatians 1:4 give clear indication of many things which are the will of God for every believer.

How may we know the will of God for specific guidance? The following steps have been very helpful in enabling believers to know God's will in specific matters.

A. Am I willing to do God's will?

"If any man will do his will, he shall know of the doctrine, whether it be of God, or whether I speak of myself" (John 7:17). Unless I am willing to do God's will once He shows it to me, why should I expect God to reveal His will to me at all? Do I want to know the will of God because I really want to do it, regardless of any cost involved? This is the first requirement in knowing God's will—a genuine willingness to do it regardless of the cost.

B. Am I surrendered?

"I beseech you therefore, brethren, by the mercies of God, that ye present your bodies a living sacrifice, holy, acceptable unto God, which is your reasonable service. And be not conformed to this world: but be ye transformed by the renewing of your mind, that ye may prove what is that good, and acceptable, and perfect will of God" (Romans 12:1,2). The Christian should ask himself, "As far as I know, have I yielded my all to Him and do not want my own way in anything?" If so, he will then be able to prove or demonstrate in his own life what is that good and acceptable and perfect will of God.

C. God works into us His will.

"For it is God which worketh in you both to will and to do of his good pleasure" (Philippians 2:13). God works into the yielded believer both the desire and the ability to do His will. He has the pattern that He desires for our lives, and He works into us His blessed and perfect will.

D. We work God's will out in our lives.

"Wherefore, my beloved . . . work out your own salvation with fear and trembling" (Philippians 2:12). What God is working into our lives, we work out by taking definite steps in the will of God as He indicates them to us. This is to be done with brokenness, humility, and fear, lest we trust ourselves in any way.

IX. The Christian Should Desire, Above All, What God Directs.

How wonderful to let the One who has infinite wisdom and love make all the choices for us. Who could possibly choose better?

Some Christians insist upon having their own will in some matters and therefore must live in just what God *permits*, not that which is His first choice. What a miserable existence this is. "He gave them their request; but sent leanness into their soul" (Psalm

106:15). Self-will in a Christian always leads to leanness of soul. The wonderful things God planned to
do must be set aside because of our self-will. "But
my people would not hearken to my voice; and
Israel would none of me. So I gave them up unto
their own hearts' lust: and they walked in their own
counsels. Oh that my people had hearkened unto
me, and Israel had walked in my ways! I should
soon have subdued their enemies, and turned my
hand against their adversaries . . . . He should have
fed them also with the finest of the wheat: and with
honey out of the rock should I have satisfied thee"
(Psalm 81:11–16).

Many Christian pastors have experienced the
heartache of seeing young people who were once
consecrated to the Lord for His service, turn back.
Instead of a life of fruitful and blessed service in the
will of God, they have gone back from the Lord into
the world, and in some cases have even married
those who were not saved.

Paul writes with real grief, "All they which are in
Asia be turned away from me; of whom are
Phygellus and Hermogenes" (II Timothy 1:15).
Later in the same epistle he speaks of Demas, his
companion, forsaking him, having chosen his own
way (II Timothy 4:10).

Desire for money certainly was not God's pathway for Ananias and Sapphira. The judgment of
death upon them was made necessary by their deceit
(Acts 5:1–11). Likewise unruliness at the Lord's
table was not God's first choice for those saints in
Corinth whose actions there had to be met with His
judgment of sickness and death (I Corinthians
11:29,30).

There are many once-valuable servants of God

who are now castaways because of their failure to keep the body under subjection (I Corinthians 9:27). Pastors and other Christian workers need to be especially careful of the Satanic onslaught which makes itself felt through appeals to the lusts of the flesh. Satan will ceaselessly attack the Christian worker along these lines. Many pastors and other church workers have succumbed to such attacks, and are now on the shelf, discredited. It is easy to count scores of such casualties among Christian workers today.

While walking near the Wissahickon Drive in Philadelphia one afternoon, I was attracted by an unfinished gas and service station. It had started out to be one of those luxurious stone buildings, but something had happened to cause construction to cease. It was now possible to peer through the broken windows and see the litter of old paper, beer cans. and other debris. God seemed to speak to my heart as I stood there. I saw this as a good picture of the Christian in whose life God once has worked but in whom the "construction" has ceased. This structure was incomplete, not because a plan was needed to complete the building, but for other reasons.

God does not stop building in a Christian's life because He has no plan for that believer, but because of the unwillingness of the believer to have God work. When self-will controls the life, then God must stop building. It may be safely said that in any life where God has stopped building, one can see the "junk" that has now come into the life. Evidences of where the builder once worked are seen too—so it is with many Christians. One can see where God has once directed, but it is also clear that God has now stopped working, and other things, never intended by God, now fill the life.

What will it be for these precious believers who have not gone on with the Lord, when they stand at His judgment seat and He judges their works? All acts done in self-will will be seen to be wood, hay, and stubble, and will be consumed by the fire of God (I Corinthians 3:12–15). What grief will come to unyielded Christians when they see what God's great purpose was for them, and then compare it to what self-will wrought in their lives.

X. The Great Rewards of Being In the Will of God.

A. The closest relationship to our Lord.
"For whosoever shall do the will of God, the same is my brother, and my sister, and mother" (Mark 3:35).

B. A life that abides forever.
"And the world passeth away, and the lust thereof: but he that doeth the will of God abideth forever" (I John 2:17).

C. Knowing the authenticity of Christ's teaching.
"If any man will do his will, he shall know of the doctrine, whether it be of God, or whether I speak of myself" (John 7:17). Knowledge of Christ depends upon honest obedience. Increased godliness always means increased knowledge of God.

D. A life of answered prayer.
"And whatsoever we ask we receive of him, because we keep his commandments, and do those things that are pleasing in his sight" (I John 3:22).

E. The companionship of One who sustains us in suffering.

Wherefore let them that suffer according to the will of God commit the keeping of their souls to him in well doing, as unto a faithful Creator" (I Peter 4:19).

F. Our life's work is not in vain.

"Therefore, my beloved brethren, be ye stedfast, unmoveable, always abounding in the work of the Lord, forasmuch as ye know that your labor is not in vain in the Lord" (I Corinthians 15:58).

May we learn from beholding the blessed example of our Lord Jesus Christ that we, too, should experience the joy of living only to know and to do God's holy and good will.

The best will is our Father's will,
    And we may rest there calm and still.
Oh! make it hour by hour thine own,
    And wish for nought but that alone
        Which pleases God.

—Paul Gerhardt, 1653

Chapter 5

BEHOLD HIM IN HIS LOVE FOR THE LOST

The prayer of each Christian should be to have a heart of love like that of Christ toward the lost. It is said of Jonathan Goforth, whom God so greatly used in China for the salvation of many souls, that he prayed this prayer each morning on his knees:

"Lord Crucified! Give me a heart like Thine;
　Teach me to love the dying souls around;
Oh, keep my heart in closest touch with Thee;
　And give me love, pure Calvary love,
　　To bring the lost to Thee."

The great need of the Christian who would be a winner of souls is to see the true condition of the lost as Christ saw it, and to love the lost as He loved them. Oh, may God grant that we may be like Christ in His great love for the lost!

I. The Great Compassion of Christ for the Lost.

"But when he saw the multitudes, he was moved with compassion on them, because they fainted, and were scattered abroad, as sheep having no shepherd" (Matthew 9:36).

What do we see when we see a crowd? A Christian

who has learned to walk with Christ will see in a crowd a multitude of souls who need a Saviour. He will be saddened at this great throng on the broad way which leads to eternal destruction. A politician sees on a crowded thoroughfare potential voters. A business man sees possible customers. An executive of a large business corporation once said, "You tell me how many people pass this storefront in one day, and I can forecast pretty accurately the yearly business of the store." He saw in people prospective purchasers.

The Lord Jesus Christ saw the multitudes as those who were in dire need spiritually. He was moved with compassion as He beheld them. It is possible that the very multitudes dead in trespasses and sins were not conscious of any need of Christ. The Holy Spirit alone can make one conscious of the need of the Saviour. Even many professed Christians are like the lukewarm church of Revelation 3:14–18, which had so much of the material luxuries of this world but was wretched, miserable, poor, blind, and naked in the eyes of Christ. Yet these people were totally unconscious of their true position before Christ and boastfully said, "I am rich, and increased with goods, and have need of nothing" (Revelation 3:17). Our compassion should go out to those who may not even be aware of their great spiritual need.

The Lord Jesus Christ could see past the self-sufficiency and false exterior of each one in the multitude. He saw their true condition apart from Him, and described it in these words, "They fainted and were scattered abroad, as sheep having no shepherd" (Matthew 9:36). They were collapsing with no source of needed spiritual strength. They were weary with nowhere to turn for succor. They had no one who was providing or planning for them. They were shepherdless, and scattered by the enemy. There could not be a more complete picture of helplessness than a sheep without a shepherd.

The scattering of the sheep speaks of the work of Satan pictured as a wolf. "The wolf catcheth them, and scattereth the sheep" (John 10:12).

When our Lord Jesus Christ saw this great needy multitude, He was moved with compassion. There was that tender pity which stirred His whole being as He beheld their helpless condition. Oh, may God give us a heart like Christ's to discern the true condition of those who are lost, and to love them!

Methods in soul winning are very helpful. It is necessary to know how to deal with the unsaved in order to show them, through the Scriptures, their sinful and lost condition. The unsaved must also realize that the penalty for their sin is eternal death. What a privilege then to reveal to them, through the Word of God, the fact that Christ was made an offering for their sin, and died on the cross for their sin. It is such a joy to show God's terms of salvation —that they must turn to Him from their sin and accept the Lord Jesus Christ as their personal Saviour and Lord.

However, the knowledge of methods in soul winning is not sufficient in itself to enable us to bring a soul to Christ. There must be above all else a Christlike heart of love and compassion for the lost. Dr. Daniel Fuchs of the American Board of Mission to the Jews conducted a brief question-and-answer period after his morning message in a church in Camden, New Jersey recently. He was asked, "What is most necessary to win a Jew to Christ?" Without hesitating in the slightest, he answered, "Love them." All the valuable training on Jewish evangelism will not avail if the Jew you are trying to lead to Christ is not conscious that you love him.

The testimony of Evan Roberts is very helpful at this point. He writes, "For thirteen years I prayed for the Spirit .... Through every kind of weather and in spite of all difficulties, I went faithfully to meetings for prayer. I prayed for revival .... In one of these meetings the evangelist petitioned the Lord to bend us. The Spirit seemed to say to me, that is what you need, to be bent. I prayed that God would bend me .... I felt a living force come into my bosom. This grew and grew. I was almost bursting. My bosom was boiling. What boiled me was the verse 'God commendeth his love' (Romans 5:8). I fell on my knees and with my arms over the seat in front, the tears and perspiration flowed freely. I thought blood was gushing forth while I cried, 'Oh, Lord, bend me, bend me.' Suddenly the glory broke. After I was bent, a wave of peace came over me, and I thought of the bending at the judgment, and I was filled with compassion for those that would have to bend on that day, and I wept. Henceforth, the burden of souls became the burden of my heart. From that time on I was on fire with a desire to go through Wales and, if possible, I was willing to pay God for the privilege of going." It was God-given compassion for the lost which made Evan Roberts the soul-winner.

II. The Lord Jesus Christ Made Social Contacts to Save People.

It is very necessary and helpful to note the social

contacts of our Lord Jesus Christ which resulted in salvation and blessing. We must learn to meet people socially, to sit where they sit, if we are to lead them to Christ and salvation. We must go out of our way to be friendly. Friendliness breaks down barriers, removes prejudices, softens resistance, and opens and prepares the hearts of people for salvation. There is a wrong and sinful isolation practiced by many of God's people.

How often, even on the way to church, the spiritually needy are passed by and no help offered. The priest and the Levite, perhaps on their way to the temple, passed by on the other side and left the stricken man half dead (Luke 10:31, 32). It would be well, when we see a needy one—even if on our way to church—to stop and minister the Word of God to him.

This is the question we should ask ourselves in all social contacts: "Why am I here?" If I am here to partake of the sin and worldliness of others, then that social contact is all wrong. However, if I am trying to win that person to Christ, then I am following His example in being social to save.

III. The Lord Jesus Christ Was Friendly With Even the Outcasts in Order to Win Them to Salvation.

It is very enlightening to consider the many outcasts our Lord won to Himself. The woman at the well came alone in the heat of the day to draw water. Why then? Likely because she was shunned by the respectable women. They usually came in the morning or evening to draw water. These times were much to be preferred in order to avoid the scorching

heat of the noonday. This woman was a sinful woman who had had five husbands, and the man with
whom she was then living was not her husband. The
Lord Jesus Christ tenderly and tactfully talked with
her. She was amazed that He, a Jew, would talk with
her, a woman of Samaria. Likewise, the apostles
marveled that He talked with the woman. The heart
of the matter is that He won this outcast to Himself.
Through her testimony, many of that city believed
on Him. It was because of "the saying of the woman
which testified, He told me all that ever I did" (John
4:39).

The Lord Jesus Christ met a maniac of Gadara,
surely an outcast. As a result of the meeting this
once wild, naked, demon-possessed man of the
tombs was found sitting and clothed, and in his right
mind. He asked that he might continue to be with
Jesus, but our Lord sent him home to his friends. He
was told to "tell how great things the Lord hath
done for thee, and hath had compassion on thee"
(Mark 5:19).

Matthew (Levi), a despised publican, was another
outcast whom the Lord approached. Jesus called
Matthew to follow Him. Our Lord's calls are always
His enablings, and Matthew "left all, rose up, and
followed him" (Luke 5:28). Then Matthew, in his
own home, made our Lord a great feast and invited
a large number of publicans and others to come. The
scribes and Pharisees murmured against His disciples,
saying, "Why do ye eat and drink with publicans
and sinners?" Our Lord answered that He was there
at that banquet as a spiritual physician attending the
spiritually sick. He said He was there at that feast to
call sinners to repentance (Luke 5:30–32).

Many professing Christians show a sinful isolation

when refusing to be social with sinners in order to win these social outcasts to Christ. We see the attitude expressed in the words of Isaiah 65:5, "Stand by thyself, come not near to me; for I am holier than thou."

Zacchaeus was of the same class of outcasts as Matthew—a publican. He was very wealthy, and much of his wealth apparently was gotten by defrauding the people. The Jews would not mingle with publicans socially. Our Lord purposely looked up in the tree where Zacchaeus, who was short of stature, was perched. He said to Zacchaeus, "Make haste, and come down, for today I must abide at thy house" (Luke 19:5). Zacchaeus hurried down and received Him joyfully. At this they all murmured saying, "He [is] gone to be guest with a man that is a sinner" (Luke 19:7).

Zacchaeus gave good evidence of a changed life by his willingness to make adequate restitution for all that was taken by false accusation. A marvelous statement was made by our Lord, "This day is salvation come to this house, forsomuch as he also is a son of Abraham" (Luke 19:9). Our Lord had won another outcast to Himself by a social contact.

All publicans and known sinners were considered to be outcasts as far as the Pharisees and scribes were concerned. When these publicans and sinners drew near to hear our Lord, these self-righteous, religious Pharisees and scribes murmured, saying, "This man receiveth sinners, and eateth with them" (Luke 15:1, 2). This remark provided the occasion for three parables of our Lord—which describe a shepherd seeking a precious lost sheep, a woman seeking a treasured lost coin, and a father seeking a lost son who was very dear to him. The point of the

three parables is not only the intense seeking for
that which was lost, but the joy in finding it. "Rejoice with me, for I have found my sheep," said
the shepherd (Luke 15:6). The woman who found
her lost coin called in all her neighbors saying, "Rejoice with me, for I have found the piece which I
had lost" (Luke 15:9). The father, upon the return
of his wayward son, said, "Let us eat and be merry,
for this my son was dead and is alive again; he was
lost and is found" (Luke 15:23,24).

These parables contain the full and complete answer of our Lord to all who would look down on
Him because of His fellowship with the so-called
outcasts of earth. He was seeking them as one who
seeks with desperate earnestness something which he
greatly values. The recovery of that which was lost
produced unspeakable joy. The outcasts of the earth
were precious in His sight and their salvation caused
Him great joy.

In our social contacts with the unpopular, we
may have to go against the current of public religious approval; but after all, what difference does
that make if we please the Lord and if the souls of
the outcasts we befriend are saved by the Lord?

A fellow pastor in the southern section of New
Jersey sought the friendship of a social outcast in
order to witness to him of Christ. He visited him
often in his self-made, ill-kept shack. Because this
man was dirty, ragged, and foul smelling, he was
avoided by the neighbors and by the town and
church people. The pastor took him in his car on
many occasions to get his necessary supplies. Otherwise this man, who was crippled, would have to
struggle on crutches one-half mile each way to and
from the store, carrying his provisions. The pastor

wrote, "It was embarrassing at first, but I determined that by the grace of God I would show him the same love I would show him if he were my father." This pastor also brought the man to his own home on Christmas. His wife and four children thus shared their blessings with him, and in a practical way demonstrated to him the love of Christ.

This is what it means to seek the social outcasts, and to love them, in order to win them to Christ. The church of Jesus Christ has too long retreated behind its beautiful walls and left alone the neighborhood of perishing people. Needy ones may be neglected when they are not on the same level socially as the people of the church.

Many a person has been won to Christ because the wise personal worker made the most of a good point of social contact. We have known of men won to Christ because someone invited them on a fishing trip, or to play horseshoes. They were invited not primarily to go fishing or to play horseshoes, but as an opportunity to love them and to show them concern, in order that they might open their hearts and receive the Saviour. Very often, sinners must first be won to us before they are won to Christ.

IV. The Lord Jesus Christ Was Constantly Seeking Individuals.

His was not just compassion in an easy chair, but a compassion which caused Him to actively seek the lost.

He announced in Zacchaeus' home that His purpose in coming into the world was to seek and to save the lost (Luke 19:10). There was an active seeking on His part of those who were lost and without hope. How we need to seek the lost. We need to have our eyes and ears open to see where God is working, and to hear the voice of the Spirit saying to us, "Go near, and join thyself to this chariot" (Acts 8:29). God uses those to win souls to Christ who are constantly seeking the lost.

In John's Gospel we have a good picture of our Lord seeking the lost. In chapter one, it is Andrew, Peter, Philip, and Nathaniel who are sought and won. These precious words describe our Lord's seeking: "The day following Jesus would go forth into Galilee, and findeth Philip, and saith unto him, Follow me" (John 1:43). We need to go forth under His direction, and find lost souls. Nicodemus is patiently won in chapter three, the woman at the well and the nobleman in chapter four, the impotent man in chapter five, the woman taken in adultery in chapter eight, and the blind man in chapter nine.

V. There Was an Urgency in the Life and Ministry of the Lord Jesus Christ.

He was conscious that He was here under a divine commission and therefore must be about God's work. This same sense of urgency is needed today by God's people. There is so much ease in Zion. Many believers, relaxing in affluence and luxury, have lost the sense of urgency. It has been said that Americans have so much to live with, and so little to live for.

Notice this divine urgency in the life of our Lord. At the age of twelve, He announced that He *must* be about His Father's business (Luke 2:49). Early in

His ministry, Peter and others would have Him tarry still longer in the place where He had performed many mighty works. He replied, "I *must* preach the kingdom of God to other cities also: for therefore am I sent" (Luke 4:43). He spoke of His cross as a *must*. "As Moses lifted up the serpent in the wilderness, even so *must* the Son of man be lifted up" (John 3:14). Just before He healed the man born blind, He said, "I *must* work the works of him that sent me, while it is day: the night cometh, when no man can work" (John 9:4). He stated, "And other sheep I have, which are not of this fold: them also I *must* bring, and they shall hear my voice; and there shall be one fold, and one shepherd" (John 10:16). He told Zacchaeus that He *must* abide in his house (Luke 19:5). God knows the very home where we must abide if there is to be salvation brought to that home. He told His disciples, who did not like to hear it, that "he *must* go unto Jerusalem, and suffer many things of the elders and chief priests and scribes, and be killed, and be raised again the third day" (Matthew 16:21). May God grant to us His servants this same sense of urgency in the work of the Lord.

VI. The Lord Jesus Christ Wept Over the Lost.

It gave the Saviour no joy to know that certain people were beyond hope of salvation and that there was ahead for them eternal destruction. He knew, as no human could ever know, the terrors of hell. It caused Him great heart sorrow when He thought of judgment upon the wicked. "And when he was come near, he beheld the city, and wept over it, saying, If thou hadst known, even thou, at least in this thy day, the things which belong unto thy peace! but now they are hid from thine eyes" (Luke 19:41,42). A heart of heaviness and sorrow over the unsaved should characterize all true believers.

The Apostle Paul had great heaviness and continual sorrow of heart because his kinsmen were not saved. He declared, "I could wish that myself were accursed from Christ for my brethren, my kinsmen according to the flesh" (Romans 9:3). It is well to note the context in which Paul made this startling statement. It contains the great passage which deals with the sovereignty of God in the salvation of the lost. "Moreover whom he did predestinate, them he also called: and whom he called, them he also justified: and whom he justified, them he also glorified" (Romans 8:30). It is very unfortunate for the evangelization of the lost that some believers have taken the position that since God has eternally decreed the salvation of whoever is to be saved, why be unduly disturbed about the lost? "The fixed decree of God cannot be altered or changed by anything we do or feel," is what they say.

The Apostle Paul, who under inspiration of the Holy Spirit wrote this passage in Romans, certainly did not share this view. His understanding of the decrees of God did not in any way prevent Paul from having such a sorrow and burden for the lost that, if it were possible, he could have wished himself accursed from Christ if this would bring salvation to those for whom he sorrowed. He also stated that it was his heart's desire and prayer to God for Israel that they might be saved (Romans 10:1). He certainly felt the unsaved should be a subject of prayer for salvation. Paul, in order to win the unsaved, was willing to endure beatings with rods, stonings, shipwrecks, and imprisonments. He was willing for the sake of the lost he wanted to win to Christ to be in danger of death daily, to be reviled, defamed, and made as the filth and offscouring of this world.

Paul's closing words to the Ephesian elders were, "Therefore watch, and remember, that by the space of three years I ceased not to warn every one night and day with tears" (Acts 20:31). If we are to win souls to Christ, we must have this God-given burden and love for the lost.

VII. The Lord Jesus Christ Would Not Soften nor Dilute His Message to the Unsaved.

The rich young ruler inquired of Christ the way to inherit eternal life. It is evident that riches were his God. He turned away sorrowful when Christ told him, "Sell all that thou hast, and distribute unto the poor, and thou shalt have treasure in heaven: and come, follow me" (Luke 18:22). We are told that "Jesus, beholding him, loved him" (Mark 10:21). Though He loved him, and wanted to save him, yet our Lord did not soften nor dilute His message even when He knew the rich young ruler would not come on the basis He stated.

This might be the appropriate place to state that the moment a Christian deliberately softens or dilutes the Word of God, that moment all hope of conviction and conversion is gone. For instance, the soul winner must not water down the message of an eternal hell for the lost. Christ ever put the warning of hell before His hearers. It is very significant that most of the teaching concerning the reality and eternity of hell comes from the lips of the Lord Jesus Christ. "I tell you, Nay: but, except ye repent, ye shall all likewise perish" (Luke 13:3,5). "Broad is the way that leadeth to destruction, and many there be which go in thereat" (Matthew 7:13). "There shall be weeping and gnashing of teeth" (Matthew 8:12). "And if thy hand offend thee, cut it off: it is better for thee to enter into life maimed, than having two hands to go into hell, into the fire that never shall be quenched" (Mark 9:43). "Depart from me, ye cursed, into everlasting fire, prepared for the devil and his angels" (Matthew 25:41).

The Christian, to be like Christ, must fearlessly declare the whole counsel of God, even though people turn away. To dilute or soften the message is fatal to soul winning.

VIII. The Lord Jesus Christ Provided Salvation at Great Cost.

There was a tremendous cost to Christ to make salvation possible. There will always be a cost to fruitfulness. The corn of wheat must fall into the ground and die before it can bring forth fruit. Christ was the corn of wheat, crucified on the cross of Calvary, whose death and resurrection made possible salvation for whosoever will. The prophet Isaiah foretold that because of the suffering on the cross "he shall see his seed" (Isaiah 53:10). Peter tells us that it was by His stripes we are healed (I Peter 2:24). He saw the travail of His soul and was satisfied because of the fruit which would come from His suffering. David wrote that because of the suffering on the cross, a seed would serve Him (Psalm 22:30).

There will be a cost to every believer who would be a soul winner. When the Apostle Paul was saved, almost the first words our Lord spoke concerning him were words telling of the deep suffering which would be connected with his privileged ministry. "He is a chosen vessel unto me, to bear my name before the Gentiles, and kings, and the children of Israel. For I will show him how great things he must suffer for my name's sake" (Acts 9:15,16). This is always the pattern: great privilege in witnessing for Christ brings with it great suffering for Christ. Paul paid the supreme sacrifice by laying down his life for Christ. He spoke of his execution as an offering: "For I am now ready to be offered" (II Timothy 4:6). His last words to Timothy and other believers were to "endure afflictions, do the work of an evangelist, make full proof of thy ministry" (II Timothy 4:5).

The Apostle Peter, after his restoration by the Lord, was told of the violent death he would die as a servant of the Lord. "This spake he, signifying by what death he should glorify God" (John 21:18,19).

There is a cost to every believer who would wholly follow the Lord. There is much suffering in the will of God (I Peter 4:19). Each believer should arm himself with a mind prepared to suffer. We are in the enemy's territory, opposed by the rulers of the darkness of this world. Careless, self-satisfied, luxury-loving Christians are not usually soul winners. It is those who pay the complete price in answering the call "Follow me" who become "fishers of men" (Matthew 4:19).

The church of Jesus Christ has largely forgotten

the word "go." "He that *goeth forth* and weepeth, bearing precious seed, shall doubtless come again with rejoicing, bringing his sheaves with him" (Psalm 126:6). The church, instead of going out after the unsaved, is hiding behind its walls, refusing to face the hardships associated with soul winning. Although we need the spiritual food and fellowship which we get by the assembling of ourselves together, this privilege does not cancel the command to go. The Holy Spirit's power was not given to the early church primarily for the church to locate in Jerusalem, but for the believers to go with the message to the ends of the earth. Paul's custom was not only to preach in the synagogues, but also in the market places and house to house. The success of the false cults is due largely to the fact that they go from house to house, relentlessly.

There is a cost to soul winning that all true believers gladly accept.

IX. Christ's Life In Us — The Key to Soul Winning.

The natural heart, because it is self-centered, has no love for the lost. It is only as the love of Christ overmasters us that we, too, are taught to love the lost. He then looks at the lost through our eyes, and yearns for them through our renewed lives. "The love of Christ constraineth us," Paul wrote in II Corinthians 5:14. The grace of God makes the labor for souls possible. "But by the grace of God I am what I am ... I labored more abundantly than they all: yet not I, but the grace of God which was with me" (I Corinthians 15:10).

It is impossible not to be a soul winner if we

wholly follow Christ. He will make us fishers of men.

Living for Jesus, through earth's little while,
    My dearest treasure the light of His smile.
Seeking the lost ones He died to redeem,
    Bringing the weary to find rest in Him.

—T. O. Chisholm.

Chapter 6

BEHOLD HIM IN HIS VICTORY
OVER THE WORLD

The victory of the Lord Jesus Christ over this anti-God, Satan-controlled world system was a complete victory.

By virtue of His holy nature, He was not of the world. He was victorious over every sinful appeal of the world. In His death upon the cross He judged the world and defeated its prince, the Devil.

It may be well at this point to discuss briefly what is meant by the expression "the world."

I. What Was the World which He Overcame?

The world is a system of which Satan is the prince. Jesus said, "The prince of this world cometh and hath nothing in me" (John 14:30). The course of this world is "according to the prince of the power of the air, the spirit that now worketh in the children of disobedience: among whom also we all had our conversation in times past in the lusts of our flesh, fulfilling the desires of the flesh and of the mind; and were by nature the children of wrath, even as others" (Ephesians 2:2,3).

Doctor C. I. Scofield has this excellent footnote

in his Reference Bible: "In the sense of the present world system, the ethically bad sense of the word refers to the order or arrangement under which Satan has organized the world of unbelieving mankind upon his cosmic principles of force, greed, selfishness, ambition, and pleasure (Matthew 4:8,9; John 12:31; 14:30; 18:36; Ephesians 2:2; 6:12; I John 2:15–17). This world system is imposing and powerful with military might; is often outwardly religious, scientific, cultured, and elegant; but, seething with national and commercial rivalries and ambitions, is upheld in any real crisis only by armed force, and is dominated by Satanic principles."*

Some characteristics of Satan's world:

1. It is a world deceived by Satan. "Satan, which deceiveth the whole world" (Revelation 12:9).

2. It is a world which lies in Satan's power. "The whole world lieth in the wicked one" (I John 5:19, margin).

3. It is a world Satanically blinded to the gospel. "The god of this world hath blinded the minds of them which believe not" (II Corinthians 4:4).

4. It is a world in which the unsaved live just for the things of this world, like the rich fool of Luke 12:16–21. "For after all these things do the Gentiles seek" (Matthew 6:32).

5. It is a world of sorrow due to sin, the final result being eternal death. "The sorrow of the world worketh death" (II Corinthians 7:10).

6. It is a world which cannot give peace of heart. "My peace I give unto you: not as the world giveth" (John 14:27).

* *The New Scofield Reference Bible* (note on Revelation 13:8)

7. It is a world which can never know God by its own wisdom. "The world by wisdom knew not God" (I Corinthians 1:21).

8. It is a world which does not know the Father, the Son, or the Holy Spirit. "O righteous Father, the world hath not known thee" (John 17:25). "He [Jesus] was in the world . . . and the world knew him not" (John 1:10). "The Spirit of truth whom the world cannot receive because it seeth him not, neither knoweth him" (John 14:17).

9. It is a world which through its sinful ignorance crucified the Lord of glory. "Which none of the princes of this world knew: for had they known it [the wisdom of God] they would not have crucified the Lord of glory" (I Corinthians 2:8).

10. It is a world which, having rejected Jesus Christ, will accept the beast when he comes. "I am come in my Father's name, and ye receive me not: if another shall come in his own name, him ye will receive" (John 5:43).

11. It is a world which hates Jesus Christ because He testified that its works are evil. "The world cannot hate you; but me it hateth, because I testify of it that the works thereof are evil" (John 7:7). The world still hates Jesus Christ.

II. By His Very Nature the Lord Jesus Christ Was Not of This World.

"And he said unto them, Ye are from beneath; I am from above: ye are of this world; I am not of this world" (John 8:23).

He was totally other than the spirit which dominated the world. Even the demons who were part of the Satanic principalities and powers recognized the Lord Jesus Christ as the Holy One of God. "What have we to do with thee, thou Jesus of Nazareth? art thou come to destroy us? I know thee who thou art, the Holy One of God" (Mark 1:24).

There was nothing defective or weak in our Lord upon which Satan, the ruler of this world's darkness, could gain a contact or a foothold. There have been imperfections in the saintliest of men—Noah, Abraham, David—but absolutely no imperfection in the Lord Jesus Christ. He was conscious His kingdom was "not of this world" (John 18:36).

III. He Announced the Fact that He Had Overcome the World.

"These things have I spoken unto you, that in me ye might have peace. In the world ye shall have tribulation: but be of good cheer; I have overcome the world" (John 16:33).

It may be asked, in what way did our Lord overcome the world?

A. He did not seek the world's empty honors.

"I receive not honor from men" (John 5:41). He did not seek the praise of fallen man, and therefore He was not affected when He did not get it. He was not bitter at man's neglect to give Him honor because He sought "the honor that cometh from God only" (John 5:44).

This was so opposite to the spirit of the world.

The desire that the natural man has for glory, praise, and position blinds his eyes to the true honor which is to be sought from God alone. How prevalent is this spirit even among us Christians. The desire to be honored of men is a very difficult desire to overcome. If a few people tell the pastor his sermon was helpful, the pastor may be so lifted up that he will not even ask himself, "Did this message please God?"

The desire to be big in the eyes of men may cause us to care little for the eyes of God.

This desire to impress men is very prominent even in those professing to serve God. The Pharisees gave alms to be seen of men, that they might have glory of men. They likewise loved to pray standing in the synagogues and in the corners of the streets that they might be seen of men. They fasted, also, in such a way that their fasting would be obvious to others (Matthew 6:1–16).

How deep must be the love for human praise when one's giving, praying, even fasting, though appearing to be for God, is really for the eyes and praise of fickle man. "For they loved the praise of men more than the praise of God" (John 12:43).

We have this same love of praise from men displayed in the desire for honorary titles. This restless desire, even among some Christians, to receive honorary degrees and to be called "Doctor" reminds us of the craving of the Pharisees to be called "Rabbi." "Diploma mills" which grant degrees on flimsy credentials have prospered, taking advantage of this innate love of praise. It may be asked, would our Lord seek such an "honor" and be restless if He did not get it?

This heart-searching question dealing with the

matter of seeking honors from men comes from the lips of our Lord: "How can ye believe, which receive honor one of another, and seek not the honor that cometh from God only?" (John 5:44). Do we really believe God if we do not seek the honor which comes only from Him? How is it possible for one who cares so much for the glory which man can bestow, to really believe on the One who rejects all such glory? It is impossible to really believe God if honor from man is also our motive.

E. M. Bounds has penned this probing paragraph: "Can ambition that lusts after praise and place preach the gospel of Him who made Himself of no reputation and took on Him the form of a servant? Can the proud, the vain, the egotistical preach the gospel of Him who was meek and lowly? Can the bad-tempered, passionate, selfish, hard, worldly man preach the system which teems with long-suffering, self-denial, tenderness, which imperatively demands separation from enmity and crucifixion to the world? Can the hireling official, heartless, perfunctory, preach the gospel which demands the Shepherd to give His life for the sheep?"*

The self-life in us clamors to be honored by men even for its "spirituality." It is quite easy to be very proud of our fine sermon on humility.

Is our spiritual life lived for the eyes of men or for the eyes of God? How often the temptation comes to the Christian to put himself and his "accomplishments" on exhibition, even while pretending to give God the glory.

The unbelieving brethren of our Lord urged Him to go immediately to the Feast of Tabernacles to display Himself. This our Lord refused (John 7:2-8).   * *Power Through Prayer*, p. 55

What God thinks of men who seek and receive such empty honors may be seen in God's judgment of Herod. Herod received such commendation after his oration that men proclaimed him to be a deity. Whether they really meant it or said it only to obtain much-needed favors from Herod is beside the point; he accepted their blasphemous adulation. "And the people gave a shout, saying, It is the voice of a god, and not of a man. And immediately the angel of the Lord smote him, because he gave not God the glory: and he was eaten of worms, and gave up the ghost" (Acts 12:22,23).

B. He fearlessly gave the world the Word of God.

"I spake openly to the world; I ever taught in the synagogue, and in the temple, whither the Jews always resort; and in secret have I said nothing" (John 18:20). He gave a fearless presentation of the Word of God as the need arose, whether it was the unmasking of the hypocrites, or a tender message to the woman at the well, or a message on the certainty of hell for the unsaved.

C. On the cross He defeated the ruler of the darkness of this world.

When the hour had come for our Lord to die upon the cross, He said, "Now is the judgment of this world: now shall the prince of this world be cast out" (John 12:31).

IV. The Believer's Victory Over the World.

The believer's victory over the world is made possible by the crucifixion of the believer with Christ to the world, and by the impartation of Christ's nature which makes the believer to be not of this world. Counting upon these two facts, the believer walks by faith and overcomes the world.

A. The crucifixion of the believer to the world.

"But God forbid that I should glory, save in the cross of our Lord Jesus Christ, by whom the world is crucified unto me, and I unto the world" (Galatians 6:14). By virtue of the believer's crucifixion with Christ, the world with its sinful domination and appeal is dead to the believer and the believer is dead to the world. Watchman Nee, in his book *Love Not the World*, writes, "Have I really seen this [the fact that the world is crucified unto us and we unto the world]? That is the question. When I see it, then I do not try to repudiate a world I love; I see that the cross *has* repudiated it. I do not try to escape a world that clings to me; I see that by the cross I *have* escaped" (p. 43).

B. The new nature makes the believer to be not of this world.

"I have given them thy word; and the world hath hated them, because they are not of the world, even as I am not of the world. I pray not that thou shouldest take them out of the world, but that thou shouldest keep them from the evil. They are not of the world, even as I am not of the world" (John 17:14–16). The divine nature makes it possible for us to escape the corruption that is in the world.

"Whereby are given unto us exceeding great and precious promises: that by these ye might be partakers of the divine nature, having escaped the corruption that is in the world through lust" (II Peter 1:4).

C. The walk of faith that overcomes the world.

"For whatsoever is born of God overcometh the world: and this is the victory that overcometh the world, even our faith. Who is he that overcometh the world, but he that believeth that Jesus is the Son of God?" (I John 5:4, 5).

D. The marks of a Christian who overcomes the world.

1. He reckons upon the fact of his crucifixion with Christ; the fact that he is dead to the world through identification with Christ in His crucifixion. He reckons upon Christ's life in him.

2. He does not seek the honor of this world. "He that loveth his life shall lose it: and he that hateth his life in this world shall keep it unto life eternal" (John 12:25).

3. He is willing to accept the hatred of men of this world. Paul was willing for Christ's sake to be as "the offscouring of all things unto this day" (I Corinthians 4:13). "If ye were of the world, the world would love his own: but because ye are not of the world, but I have chosen you out of the world, therefore the world hateth you" (John 15:19).

4. He learns not to be conformed to this world. "And be not conformed to this world: but be ye transformed by the renewing of your mind, that ye may prove what is that good, and acceptable, and perfect will of God" (Romans 12:2). The Christian learns that "friendship of the world is enmity with God" (James 4:4). The Christian is taught by the Lord "to keep himself unspotted from the world" (James 1:27).

5. He learns to set his affection on things above, not on things of this world. "If ye then be risen with Christ, seek those things which are above, where Christ sitteth on the right hand of God. Set your affection on things above, not on things on the earth" (Colossians 3:1,2).

It seems that the key verses in the Bible regarding the Christian and his attitude to the world are found in I John 2:15–17: "Love not the world, neither the things that are in the world. If any man love the world, the love of the Father is not in him. For all that is in the world, the lust of the flesh, and the lust of the eyes, and the pride of life, is not of the Father, but is of the world. And the world passeth away, and the lust thereof: but he that doeth the will of God abideth forever."

6. He lives in this world by the grace of God, not by fleshly wisdom. "For our rejoicing is this, the testimony of our conscience, that in simplicity and godly sincerity, not with fleshly wisdom, but by the grace of God, we have had our conversation in the world, and more abundantly toward you" (II Corinthians 1:12).

7. He gives the message of salvation to a dying world by his life and word. "Ye are the light of the world. A city that is set on an hill cannot be hid. ... Let your light so shine before men, that they may see your good works, and glorify your Father which is in heaven" (Matthew 5:14, 16). "As thou hast sent me into the world, even so have I also sent them into the world" (John 17:18).

May it be our blessed experience to be like Christ and be overcomers of this sin-cursed, Satan-controlled world.

Earthly pleasures vainly call me,
    I would be like Jesus;
Nothing worldly shall enthrall me,
    I would be like Jesus.

—James Rowe

Chapter 7

BEHOLD HIM IN HIS VICTORY OVER SATAN

It is impossible for any Christian to be triumphant in his personal life and ministry unless he is aware of God's provision for victory over the power of Satan. The Christian must understand and appropriate for himself the victory of Christ on the cross over Satan and the powers of darkness, or he will never know what a life of victory is.

There is a great deal of ignorance even among true believers regarding Satan. This should not be. The Apostle Paul wrote, "Lest Satan should get an advantage of us: for we are not ignorant of his devices" (II Corinthians 2:11). The Christian should not be ignorant of Satan's devices or Satan will surely be in a position of advantage.

Some professing Christians even go so far as to deny Satan's existence. The late Pastor O. R. Palmer of Berachah Church of Philadelphia wrote in 1934 that the results of a questionnaire sent to fifteen hundred ministers showed that 54% did not believe there was a personal devil. It would not be surprising if the percentage were even higher now. How powerless such so-called ministers would be to meet a Satanic onslaught, and how impotent they would be to lead others into a life of victory over Satan.

God would have us learn from the Scriptures of the origin of Satan, his tremendous power and evil designs, and his crushing defeat at the cross.

I. Satan's Origin and Tremendous Power.

A. Satan's Origin.

In his unfallen state Satan was named Lucifer, which means "son of the morning" or "bright shining one" (Isaiah 14:12). It closely resembles the name "bright morning star." He was "the anointed cherub that covereth" (Ezekiel 28:14). He was perhaps the guardian of the very throne of God. He was "full of wisdom and perfect in beauty" (Ezekiel 28:12). His heart was lifted up with pride when he became occupied with himself and with his beauty. This led to his revolt against God. He had become dissatisfied, even with all that God had made him, and he desired to be greater. He no longer was content with the place where God had put him. Five times in defiance he said "I will" to God, as recorded in Isaiah 14:13,14.

1. "I will ascend into heaven."

He aspired to be in the very place where God ruled.

2. "I will exalt my throne above the stars of God."

He had a throne given him but there was an area in which he was not supreme, where he was determined to be the ruler. It was a height far above the power of other creatures to penetrate.

3. "I will sit also upon the mount of the congregation, in the sides of the north."

The mount of the congregation, it is thought, was the place of assembling of all the angelic hosts, where

they gathered to worship their Creator. Lucifer
aspired to sit there with himself as the object of
worship.

4. "I will ascend above the heights of the
clouds."

The cloud was the symbol of the divine glory
(Exodus 13:21). Lucifer purposed to be above the
glory clouds of the triune Jehovah.

5. "I will be like the Most High."

He aimed to be as God, and he aimed to have the
worship which belongs to God alone.

His purposes have not changed over the centuries.
He still demands to be worshiped as God. The worship of Satan is already being practiced on an increasing scale in different parts of the world.

A wedding took place in San Francisco on Janu-
ary 31, 1967 performed by a so-called priest of
Satan, as reported in the *Camden Courier* February
1, 1967. Asking the blessing of Lucifer and Beelze-
bub, the priest of Satan performed the marriage ceremony using a naked woman as an altar. Anton
LaVey, who bills himself as the first priest of the
Satanic Church, said he concocted the ceremony
from his fifteen-year study of witchcraft, sorcery,
and Satanism. LaVey said his diabolic work is thriv-
ing.

This priest of Satan had his little daughter "baptized" for Satan. The following is from an article in
Watching and Waiting:

Little Zeena Galatea LaVey became a full-
fledged witch last night . . . . Her lovely blonde
mummy is already a witch. And her daddy,
Anton, is the self-styled Sorcerer and High Priest
of the first Satanic Church . . . . Zeena seemed to

love every minute of this devilish family "baptism." She sat at the feet of a naked woman who was stretched out on a leopardskin-covered "altar" with a flower behind her ear. Zeena's father, dressed up in a black cloak and hood topped by a pair of plastic horns, touched her on the head with a sword. Then he anointed her with earth, fire (a candle flame), and water . . . . The Satanic "baptism" was the second public ceremony conducted in the ritual chamber of the devil worshipers' church, which is also the LaVey's two-story house in San Francisco. The first, in February, was a "black wedding." During the ceremony, Anton rang a bell and intoned: "Welcome Zeena, blessed sister witch. We dedicate your life to passion and indulgence."

A reporter from the *Camden Courier* was permitted to visit a meeting where Satanism is practiced in Camden County, New Jersey. The following is taken from his report which was published September 3, 1968:

> Witchcraft—or Satanism, if you will—is being practiced right here in Camden County!
> The leader said, "We don't worship or practice evil—but we do glorify Satan and the lusts of the flesh . . . . Actually, a worship of the devil is more in keeping with the times in which we live anyhow," the warlock said. "By their practices, most people apparently worship the devil, only they refuse to admit it."
> The liturgy begins—which consists of sacrilegious treatments of common prayers, with the substitution of "Satan" for "God," and readings from Milton's *Paradise Lost*, Dante's *Inferno*, and some obscure poems.

After more incense, the new member, who is also naked, is brought into the circle. First she is asked to deny God and to pledge allegiance to Satan—which she does . . . . Although most of the ritual is in the hands of the head warlock, the most important is the head witch, who comes into the circle anointed with a perfumed oil and is symbolically the bride of Satan.

Christianity Today, in an editorial "Demonism on the March" appearing in the February 17, 1967 issue, gives us this information:

Demonism is a growing phenomenon throughout the world. The news media report its rapid spread in England. We have been told that Germany now has more witches, wizards, and necromancers than full-time Christian workers. An American pastor with a German-born wife recently described the case of two demon-possessed, black-attired girls "baptized to Satan." Their parents are demon-worshipers . . . . Demonism today is a further manifestation of man's revolt against God.

The Apostle Paul tells us that when the man of sin, the son of perdition is revealed, he will exalt himself above all that is called God, or that is worshiped; and that he will sit as God in the temple of God, "showing himself that he is God" (II Thessalonians 2:4).

The Apostle John tells us of the time when all the unsaved world will worship the beast. "And all that dwell upon the earth shall worship him, whose names are not written in the book of life of the Lamb slain from the foundation of the world" (Revelation 13:8). "As many as would not worship the image of the beast should be killed" (Revelation 13:15).

The holiness of God demanded an immediate judgment upon Lucifer's rebellion in heaven. "How art thou fallen from heaven, O Lucifer" (Isaiah 14:12). The Lord Jesus Christ declared, "I beheld Satan as lightning fall from heaven" (Luke 10:18).

Lucifer became Satan which means "adversary." He is the adversary of God, and all that is for God's glory.

B. Satan's Tremendous Power.

Satan retains tremendous power and cunning, and has had thousands of years of experience in dealing with the individuals of the human race.

He seems to be almost omnipresent, being able to assault people throughout the world. A vast host of demons, subject to him, enables him to exercise this tremendous diabolical power.

1. Satan is the head of all evil principalities and powers. The fallen angels who with him rebelled against God are aligned with him, as are a vast host of demons. Demons can cause blindness, dumbness (Matthew 12:22, Luke 11:14), immorality (Mark 1:23), insanity (Mark 5:15). They are very cruel and merciless (Luke 9:39).

2. Satan is the ruler of the darkness of this world. He is the god of this age (II Corinthians 4:4), the prince of this world (John 14:30). He is "prince of the power of the air, the spirit that now worketh in the children of disobedience" (Ephesians 2:2). The whole world lieth in the evil one (I John 5:19).

The Satanic rulership of the world is accomplished by a highly organized system of demons and evil spirits who not only control the unsaved but who have access to the rulers of the world, and are able to influence decisions of world leaders.

We see this clearly in the preparation for the future battle of Armageddon: "And I saw three unclean spirits like frogs come out of the mouth of the dragon, and out of the mouth of the beast, and out of the mouth of the false prophet. For they are the spirits of demons, working miracles, which go forth unto the kings of the earth and of the whole world, to gather them to the battle of that great day of God Almighty" (Revelation 16:13,14).

Rulers of the world may feel that they are making their own independent decisions, based on the necessity of the world situation, as they see it. However, all unknown to them, their decisions can be traced directly to the influence of demons carrying out the express wishes of the dragon, the beast, and the false prophet.

There is a very interesting record in Daniel 10:2–14 which may throw more light on the involvement of demons in the affairs of nations. Daniel, a man beloved of God, had mourned and fasted for three weeks. Daniel was one whose heart was exercised with the welfare of God's people. The more a man walks with God, the more concern and sorrow he has for wayward people of God. Daniel greatly desired that the Jewish captives taken to Babylon would return to Jerusalem and Judah, as Cyrus' decree had made possible. Daniel was grieved that few cared to return. Many preferred the ease in sinful Babylon. They had no heart interest in the things of God. This was the awful state of the people through whom God had chosen to work in the world.

Daniel, deeply burdened, turned to the Lord in prayer. This prayer of Daniel seemed so different from his usual prayers because no answer came. His previous prayer was answered while he was yet praying (Daniel 9:20–22). But now, for three weeks there had been constant prayer but no answer.

Finally Daniel was very graciously granted a vision of the Lord Jesus Christ. The vision comforted and strengthened him, but there was still no answer to his prayer. Then an angel touched him and told him the reason for the delay.

From the first day that Daniel set his heart to understand and to chasten himself before God, his prayer was heard. The angel was sent to bring Daniel the answer, but the prince of the kingdom of Persia withstood the angel twenty-one days until the Archangel Michael came to help him get the answer through to Daniel.

Who, then, is this wicked personality who has access to the unseen spirit world and who definitely opposed all that God willed for His people? This personality is more than a mere man. No man of earth, no matter how powerful, can recognize and withstand an angel of God. So great and powerful was the prince of Persia that he knew of the angel's coming with the answer to Daniel's prayer, and was able to hold the angel back for three weeks, and only gave way when Michael came to help.

This prince of Persia (Persia had conquered Babylon) could only be one of these Satanic emissaries, a demon—a demon prince who was assigned by Satan to rule in Persia in league with the powers of darkness. He resented and opposed any prayer that would loosen Satan's hold on Persia.

3. Satan has his own ministers and false prophets. Someone has well said, "When searching to see the extent of the power of the devil, do not fail to look in the pulpit." The Scriptures abound with the teaching that Satan will have his counterfeits posing as real servants of God.

Paul wrote, "For such are false apostles, deceitful workers, transforming themselves into the apostles of Christ. And no marvel; for Satan himself is transformed into an angel of light. Therefore it is no great thing if his ministers also be transformed as the ministers of righteousness; whose end shall be according to their works" (II Corinthians 11:13-15).

The Lord Jesus Christ left us a warning, saying, "Take heed that no man deceive you. For many shall come in my name, saying, I am Christ; and shall deceive many . . . . For there shall arise false Christs, and false prophets, and shall show great signs and wonders; insomuch that, if it were possible, they shall deceive the very elect. Behold, I have told you before" (Matthew 24:4, 5, 24, 25).

4. Satan has his own doctrines and practices.

a. He casts doubt on the word spoken by God.

One of the practices of the devil, revealed early in the Bible, is to cast doubt upon the word which God had spoken. Satan said, "Yea, hath God said, Ye shall not eat of every tree of the garden?" (Genesis 3:1).

b. He denies the word of God.

In tempting Eve, Satan denied that death is the wages of sin. The serpent said to the woman, "Ye shall not surely die" (Genesis 3:4). God had said, "In the day that thou eatest thereof thou shalt surely die" (Genesis 2:17).

c. He perverts the Scriptures.

He knows at least the words of Scripture but perverts the meaning of Bible passages which he uses. This has been previously cited, when in the temptation of our Lord (Matthew 4:6) Satan purposely omitted a vital clause in quoting to our Lord from Psalm 91:11 and 12.

Representatives of false cults come with the Bible in their hands, but also with another book, or books, which pervert the teaching of the Bible—such as *Science and Health with Key to the Scriptures*, and the many Watchtower publications.

Satan is the great perverter of Scripture, which he twists and turns to accomplish his own purposes.

d. He rejects the necessity of Christ's death upon the cross.

"From that time forth began Jesus to show unto his disciples how that he must go unto Jerusalem, and suffer many things of the elders and chief priests and scribes, and be killed, and be raised again the third day. Then Peter took him, and began to rebuke him, saying, Be it far from thee, Lord: this shall not be unto thee. But he turned, and said unto Peter, Get thee behind me, Satan: thou art an offense unto me" (Matthew 16:21–23).

The Lord Jesus Christ recognized the voice of Satan speaking through Peter. Satan was trying to persuade Christ that it was not necessary for Him to go to the cross and that this idea should be far from Him.

One can detect, likewise, in the voices of those about the cross, the hatred of the devil for the offering of the blood of Christ. Even before the victorious sacrifice was completed, they cried for Him to come down from the cross. "If he be the King of Israel, let him now come down from the cross, and we will believe him" (Matthew 27:42).

The Satanic hatred of the shed blood of the Lord Jesus Christ and the finished work of the cross is seen in the preaching of Satan's ministers. "But there were false prophets also among the people, even as there shall be false teachers among you, who privily shall bring in damnable heresies, even denying the Lord that bought them and bring upon themselves swift destruction" (II Peter 2:1).

The denial of the Lord who bought them is the denial of the purchase price, the precious blood of the Lord Jesus Christ shed on the cross.

e. He denies the resurrection of the Lord Jesus Christ.

Satan, who is a liar and the father of liars, inspired the lie denying the resurrection. "And when they were assembled with the elders, and had taken counsel, they gave large money unto the soldiers, saying, Say ye, His disciples came by night, and stole him away while we slept" (Matthew 28:12,13).

f. Deception is the great characteristic of Satan.

Eve's sad confession, as she faced the Lord was, "The serpent beguiled me, and I did eat" (Genesis 3:13).

Paul wrote, "The woman being deceived was in the transgression" (I Timothy 2:14).

"If it were possible, they shall deceive the very elect," were Christ's words regarding the false prophets (Matthew 24:24).

When the beast makes his appearance, his coming

will be "after the working of Satan with all power and signs and lying [deceptive] wonders" (II Thessalonians 2:9).

Satan "deceiveth the whole world" (Revelation 12:9). Millions upon the earth who will receive the mark of the beast will do so because they will have been deceived. "And the beast was taken, and with him the false prophet that wrought miracles before him, with which he deceived them that had received the mark of the beast, and them that worshipped his image. These both were cast alive into a lake of fire burning with brimstone" (Revelation 19:20).

These false doctrines of Satan are called the doctrines of demons. These erroneous doctrines are taught by demons to unregenerate, spiritually blind false prophets and teachers. "Now the Spirit speaketh expressly, that in the latter times some shall depart from the faith, giving heed to seducing spirits, and doctrines of demons" (I Timothy 4:1).

These false teachers will guide a vast multitude of people into these false doctrines. "And many shall follow their pernicious ways; by reason of whom the way of truth shall be evil spoken of" (II Peter 2:2).

The sad result will be that "if the blind lead the blind, both shall fall into the ditch" (Matthew 15:14).

5. The last form of the organized church on earth will be a demon-possessed church.

"And he cried mightily with a strong voice, saying, Babylon the great is fallen, is fallen, and is become the habitation of demons, and the hold of every foul spirit, and a cage of every unclean and hateful bird" (Revelation 18:2). This church is what will be left on earth after the true believers, the born-again ones, the body of Christ, are caught away at the rapture to be with the Lord.

The Ecumenical Movement, uniting outwardly all Protestant churches and looking forward to union with Roman Catholicism, is preparing the way for this world church which Scripture calls "the great whore that sitteth upon many waters" (Revelation 17:1).

II. Satan and the Sinner.

It may be well to add a further word concerning the tremendous power of Satan over the individual sinner.

Scripture tells us that "the god of this world hath blinded the minds of them which believe not, lest the light of the glorious gospel of Christ, who is the image of God, should shine unto them" (II Corinthians 4:4).

The unsaved walk "according to the prince of the power of the air [Satan]" (Ephesians 2:2). It is Satan's spirit which is now working in the children of disobedience. Sinners are helpless to escape; they are under the power of Satan (Acts 26:18). They are of their father the devil (John 8:44). "He that committeth sin is of the devil" (I John 3:8). "The tares are the children of the wicked one" (Matthew 13:38).

Satan is merciless and cruel, oppressing and afflicting his captives. He does all within his power to keep them from salvation, even snatching away the Word of God, lest it take root in their hearts and bring forth salvation (Mark 4:15).

The broad way which leads to destruction and to

eternal hell is filled with those who have been blinded and deceived by the devil.

The question may be asked, who then shall be able to overcome such a malignant and powerful foe?

III. The Superior Power of the Lord Jesus Christ.

The Lord Jesus Christ, during His earthly life, exercised His authority over all the powers of darkness. Demons had to obey His liberating word. They had to recognize His holiness and submit to His orders.

The Lord Jesus Christ accepted no praise or adoration from the powers of darkness.

There was a man with an unclean spirit in the synagogue, and the spirit in him cried out, "Let us alone; what have we to do with thee, thou Jesus of Nazareth? art thou come to destroy us? I know thee who thou art, the Holy One of God." And Jesus rebuked him, saying, "Hold thy peace, and come out of him" (Mark 1:24,25).

"Unclean spirits, when they saw him, fell down before him, and cried, saying, Thou art the Son of God. And he straitly charged them that they should not make him known" (Mark 3:11,12).

He set the maniac of Gadara free from the demons which had held him in cruel bondage (Mark 5:5–15).

He set Mary Magdalene free from the harassing possession of seven demons (Luke 8:2).

It is evident therefore that the Lord Jesus Christ during His life on earth clearly demonstrated His superiority over all the powers of darkness.

IV. The Victory on the Cross of the Lord Jesus
    Christ Over Satan.

The victory over Satan and his evil dominions was
first promised immediately after the fall of man into
sin. The Lord God said to Satan, "I will put enmity
between thee and the woman, and between thy seed
and her seed; it shall bruise thy head, and thou shalt
bruise his heel" (Genesis 3:15).

Here is the definite promise that the seed of the
woman would deal the serpent the crushing blow of
defeat. This crushing defeat was to be accomplished
on the cross. As the time drew near for the crucifixion, our Lord announced the victory which
would be won because of His cross: "Now is the
judgment of this world: now shall the prince of this
world be cast out. And I, if I be lifted up from the
earth, will draw all men unto me. This he said, signifying what death he should die" (John 12:31-33).

Our Lord once asked a question in order to make
it clear how to set free Satanic captives. "How can
one enter into a strong man's house and spoil his
goods, except he first bind the strong man? and then
he will spoil his house" (Matthew 12:29).

Satan may be likened to a strong man, armed,
who guards his spoils, the captive souls. If the souls
held captive are ever to be delivered, the strong man
must be dealt with effectively. He must be rendered
powerless. He must be bound.

The Lord Jesus Christ bound the strong man by
means of His death and resurrection. Now our Lord
can set Satan's captives free.

He shouted the cry of victory on the cross when
He cried, "It is finished" (John 19:30). The perfect
tense of the Greek verb indicates both the fact that

the task was finished and that the effect of what was finished continues on. So on the cross the Lord Jesus Christ defeated Satan, and all the powers of darkness, and the effect of this victory will continue on throughout the countless ages of eternity.

"The Son of God was manifested that he might destroy the works of the devil" (I John 3:8). Satan met a total defeat by the death of the Lord Jesus Christ on the cross. "Forasmuch then as the children are partakers of flesh and blood, he also himself likewise took part of the same; that through death he might destroy him that had the power of death, that is, the devil; and deliver them who through fear of death were all their lifetime subject to bondage" (Hebrews 2:14,15).

"And having spoiled principalities and powers, he made a show of them openly, triumphing over them in it" (Colossians 2:15).

Satan, the archenemy of God and of all right-eousness, is now a defeated foe. The Lord Jesus Christ, having defeated Satan, can set the captives free from Satan's bondage.

How wonderfully the Lord sets the captives free. He first convicts of sin through the operation of the Holy Spirit, and then enables the one dead in sin to lay hold of and accept Jesus Christ as Saviour and Lord.

Jesus announced as His purpose, "He hath anointed me to preach the gospel to the poor; he hath sent me to heal the broken-hearted, to preach deliverance to the captives, and recovering of sight to the blind, to set at liberty them that are bruised" (Luke 4:18).

The saved sinner may now rejoice that he has been delivered from the power of darkness and has been translated into the kingdom of God's dear Son (Colossians 1:13).

"But ye are a chosen generation, a royal priesthood, an holy nation, a peculiar people; that ye should show forth the praises of him who hath called you out of darkness into his marvelous light" (I Peter 2:9).

V. Satan and the Saint.

Even though Satan is now a defeated foe, nevertheless, he still exercises tremendous power against the saints of God. He marshals all of the powers of darkness against them.

"For we wrestle not against flesh and blood, but against principalities, against powers, against the rulers of the darkness of this world, against spiritual wickedness in high places" (Ephesians 6:12). Wrestling is a form of athletic competition in which the combatants are locked together in the closest form of physical conflict. This gives us some idea of the closeness of the conflict of Satan with the saint.

A knowledge of Satan's program against the saint is essential. Paul said concerning Satan, "We are not ignorant of his devices" (II Corinthians 2:11). It would be well if every saint could say this. These are some of the devices Satan uses against Christians:

1. He tempts Christians to a life of independence from God (Matthew 4:1–11).

2. He tempts Christians to act in such a way as to make the labor of God's workers vain (I Thessalonians 3:5).

3. He tempts Christians to lean on the arm of flesh, and depend on statistics rather than upon God (I Chronicles 21:1–7).

4. He tempts Christians to depart from a life of simple faith in Christ (II Corinthians 11:3). Satan beguiled Eve through telling her she needed some superior religious experience which disobedience to God would produce. How many Christians have departed from the simplicity of a life of faith in Christ by seeking some so-called superior religious experience.

5. He hinders Christians from making needy visits (I Thessalonians 2:18).

6. He seeks to wear out the saints with worry (I Peter 5:7,8; Daniel 7:25).

7. He seeks to get the Christian to oppose the program of God. Satan tried to persuade Christ not to go to the cross, speaking through the Apostle Peter. Satan can speak to us through our close associates, even as he spoke to Christ through Peter (Matthew 16:22,23).

8. He desires to destroy the Christian's faith (Luke 22:31). This is why our Lord prayed that under Satan's attack Peter's faith would not fail.

9. He desires to get the Christian to lift up his heart in pride (I Timothy 3:6,7).

10. He tries to get every advantage of the Christian (II Corinthians 2:11).

11. He desires to buffet the Christian and make him discouraged, and cause him to turn back from the work of the Lord. But God can overrule any Satanic buffeting for His glory and our good (II Corinthians 12:7,8; Romans 8:28).

12. He can influence the Christian to lie to the Holy Ghost (Acts 5:3).

These are just a few of the devices of Satan which he uses to render the Christian defeated, unfruitful, discouraged, and faithless. Satan pressures the Christian to turn back to the world with its lust of the flesh, lust of the eyes, and pride of life. It is to be feared that many Christians have become castaways by succumbing to Satan's power (I Corinthians 9:27).

VI. The Saint's Victory Over Satan.

It may well be asked, how can a Christian possibly enjoy constant victory over such a wicked, powerful foe as Satan?

The secret of victory for the Christian is to appropriate and rest in the victory of our Lord Jesus Christ, which He won on the cross. The tribulation saints demonstrate for us this secret of victory: "And they overcame him [Satan] by the blood of the Lamb, and by the word of their testimony; and they loved not their lives unto the death" (Revelation 12:11).

The blood of the Lamb represents the victory won by our Lord on the cross. The intelligent use of Christ's victory, in a situation where Satan attacks, is God's program for those who would be overcomers.

These believers in Revelation 12, under the direct personal attack of Satan, by faith applied the victory of the cross to the Satanic attack and they overcame. The method is somewhat like this: When Satan is attacking or has already gotten a temporary victory, and the work of God is suffering loss, it is good for the Christian warrior to go alone with the Lord and lay in detail the whole matter before Him. It is then good for the Christian to remind himself of passages of Scripture which reveal that Satan is a defeated foe. For the glory of God, he can then claim that the victory won on the cross shall be made effective in the present situation. This is to be done in complete surrender. "They loved not their lives unto the death."

The whole matter is then rested with the Lord in complete confidence that Satan's hold has been broken. This prayer will at times be in agony and much exercise of soul. The Holy Spirit in our weakness will lead us in appropriating this victory of Christ on the cross over Satan and the powers of darkness.

In many years of ministry we have been subjected to many Satanic attacks. Human resources failed. Supernatural power was needed. We have experienced glorious victory in each instance when we claimed the victory which our Lord won on the cross over the powers of darkness.

It is in our utter helplessness that we learn to overcome Satan by the blood of the Lamb. Paul tells us explicitly, "The weapons of our warfare are not carnal, but mighty through God to the pulling down of strongholds" (II Corinthians 10:4).

No amount of human genius, logic, persuasion, or plans can defeat Satan. The grandest of all carnal weapons are doomed to fail. There is no mightier weapon than the blood of the Lamb.

Many Christians needlessly suffer constant defeat and cruel oppression from Satan because of failure to make use of the victory of Christ over Satan on the cross. So often Christians make an effort to lessen the effects of Satan's attacks, whereas God would have us deal with and be victorious over Satan himself. We are in spiritual combat, and we need intelligent, determined action on the spiritual battlefield if we are to be victorious. We must be clothed with the armor of God to face the awful foe. There is no safety in fleeing; there is no armor provided for the back of the warrior. Safety is in facing the foe, clothed in the armor of God, strong in His victory.

"Finally, my brethren, be strong in the Lord, and in the power of his might. Put on the whole armor of God, that ye may be able to stand against the wiles of the devil. For we wrestle not against flesh and blood, but against principalities, against powers, against the rulers of the darkness of this world, against spiritual wickedness in high places. Wherefore take unto you the whole armor of God, that ye may be able to withstand in the evil day, and having done all, to stand" (Ephesians 6:10–13).

Satan is to be resisted by the Christian. "Submit yourselves therefore to God. Resist the devil, and he will flee from you" (James 4:7). "Be sober, be vigilant; because your adversary the devil, as a roaring lion, walketh about seeking whom he may devour: whom resist stedfast in the faith" (I Peter 5:8,9).

The Apostle Paul, in his letter to the Romans, makes a statement which should be the experience of every Christian: "And the God of peace shall bruise Satan under your feet shortly" (Romans 16:20).

God must do the bruising of Satan for us. We are powerless in ourselves to obtain any victory over Satan and the powers of darkness. However, it is to be under our feet where the bruising is to take place. In our circumstances, in our situation, God enforces the victory of the cross over Satan's attacks.

These words of the Apostle Paul remind one of Joshua's invitation to the captains of the men of war: "Come near, put your feet upon the necks of these kings. And they came near, and put their feet upon the necks of them" (Joshua 10:24).

Joshua had won the victory over these five kings and their armies because the Lord delivered them into his hands (Joshua 10:8). The defeated kings fled and hid in a cave. Joshua sealed the cave with great stones while the defeated armies of these kings were pursued and destroyed by the children of Israel. Then Joshua ordered these kings out of the cave, and invited his captains to put their feet upon the necks of these defeated kings.

In a similar way, our triumphant Joshua, the Lord Jesus Christ, has won the victory over Satan. He longs to have us share in His triumph. He makes it possible for us to share His conquest, and invites us to appropriate and use it in faith.

His tremendous victory provides the only way for us to live triumphantly over Satan.

May it be our constant experience in our combat with Satan and the powers of darkness that our victorious Lord is constantly bruising Satan under our feet.

Just a further word may be in order about the absolute necessity of appropriating and standing in this victory of our Lord on the cross. It is blessedly true that the provision is in our conquering Christ: "Ye are of God, little children, and have overcome them: because greater is he that is in you, than he that is in the world" (I John 4:4). This is true of every believer: "Greater is he that is in you, than he that is in the world." Yet even with a Greater than Satan in us, it is possible for a Christian to go down in defeat.

Every defeated Christian has One within who is

greater in power than Satan, the one who is defeating him at the moment. However, we must face the Satanic attack in the full application of our Lord's victory. By faith we must rest our case there if we are ever to enjoy a life of triumph.

It is a great joy to know that our Lord did on the cross all that was necessary for our victory. But is it right for us to fold our hands complacently and say, "All has been done on Calvary"? No, we must lay hold of this victory; we must claim it by faith.

May God teach us increasingly how to stand in His triumph.

> Soldiers of Christ, arise,
>   And put your armor on,
> Strong in the strength which God supplies
>   Through His eternal Son;
> Strong in the Lord of Hosts,
>   And in His mighty power,
> Who in the strength of Jesus trusts
>   Is more than conqueror.
>
> —Charles Wesley

SCRIPTURE INDEX

Scripture Index